Contents

LL

SELF-EMPLOYMENT

The Essential Guide

ances Ive

Self-Employment – The Essential Guide is also available in accessible formats for people with any degree of visual impairment. The large print edition and eBook (with accessibility features enabled) are available from Need2Know. Please let us know if there are any special features you require and we will do our best to accommodate your needs.

First published in Great Britain in 2011 by
Need2Know
Remus House
Coltsfoot Drive
Peterborough
PE2 9BF
Telephone 01733 898103
Fax 01733 313524
www.need2knowbooks.co.uk

Introduction

One of the best options when jobs are scarce is to start up a business of your own. This can be anything from offering your skills to the public or businesses, providing a service locally or nationally, running a commercial website, producing or selling products, or taking on a franchise.

Freedom, flexibility, being your own boss and being in control of your own destiny are some of the key reasons why people choose to go self-employed. More and more women work for themselves, as part-time jobs become harder to find, and because it enables them to organise their work around family life.

A survey recently found that 49% of Britons think that this is an entrepreneurial country, and that over one third (34%) either want to or already have started their own business. Of these, 58% said their main reason for wanting to be self-employed was 'being their own boss', followed by 54% saying they wanted to 'reap all the rewards of my own hard work' and 43% claiming 'I want to make more money'.

Despite difficult economic times, self-employment started to grow in the 1980s partly due to changing social attitudes and the diminishing chance of finding a 'job for life'. Nowadays it isn't much more risky than working for an organisation, as redundancies can strike at any time. So do the benefits of self-employment outweigh the downsides?

Working for yourself should not be considered an easy option, so you should take plenty of time to think about what you are going to do and how. A self-employed person is responsible for the success of the business, and at times it can get lonely, particularly if you are used to working in a team or around other people. It is essential to decide if you can cope with the peaks and troughs of work, emotional ups and downs, unstable financial income and not having anyone else to bounce ideas off if you are working alone.

'The day that I started working for myself was a great moment in my life. Wild horses wouldn't get me back to working for someone else again, never in a million years. That independence, that feeling of self-preservation is fantastic.'

Lord Sugar from the programme, *Piers meets Lord Sugar*, ITV. Alan Sugar started working for himself with £100 and is now a multi-millionaire!

A lot of people who start off self-employed, work with a partner or run a small company. Alternatively, they may start off small and grow, while others remain as sole traders throughout their career. There are a variety of choices about how you operate and whether or not you form a partnership, a limited company or operate on your own as a sole trader.

When self-employment became popular in the 1980s the economy was sound, pay was good and more and more people decided it was the way they wanted to work. It suited companies too because it meant that they didn't need to take on full-time staff for whom they had to provide holiday and sickness pay, and National Insurance contributions. Companies can outsource work or find freelancers when they have busy periods, and lay them off when they are going through a quiet time

Times are tough and dole queues are growing, so more people will choose self-employment. The good news is that there is plenty of help and advice out there, and many different types to consider. This book helps to provide you with an overview of all the things you need to take into account when becoming self-employed, with pointers to where to find practical help and guidance.

Chapter One

Why Do You Want To Be Self-employed?

Every year, more and more people become self-employed for a variety of reasons, one of which is the state of the economy. Finding a job in difficult times can take so long that some people decide to set up on their own, either doing what they are experienced in or opting for something new.

The flexibility of self-employment means that you can choose to do more than one thing, combining different careers or keeping a part-time job to be sure that money is coming in while setting up a new business. Within some industries being self-employed is very common – journalists, teachers and consultants often work for themselves, while for electricians, builders, plumbers and the like, it is the norm.

Redundancy

Redundancy often enables people to opt for self-employment, particularly if they have been given a payout which tides them over the early months and helps them to start up. People who choose the industry that they have already worked in, have the skills and expertise needed to operate in that area and often have contacts who can give them work and get them started.

'Finding a job in difficult times can take so long that some people decide to set up on their own, either doing what they are experienced in or opting for something new.'

Having a family

Working as a self-employed person or a freelancer, is often a lifestyle choice, and a particularly suitable one for women who have a family. Being self-employed enables you to be around for your children and still earn money. It also means that you can spend more time at home, less time commuting and you can be flexible and work the hours that suit you.

More and more women are choosing to be self-employed and there are plenty of good reasons for that. Some provide a much-needed second income in the family, while others do not need to work financially but want the stimulation of work. For single parents, the time and money saved in not having to travel to work enables them to fulfil commitments like picking up the children from school, doing the shopping and keeping on top of household jobs at home.

> ## Case study
>
> 'I love being self-employed. As a mother it's great because work is so flexible: you can be at sports day for your children without having to ask for the afternoon off and just make up the time in the evening. And if the kids are suddenly taken ill you don't have to make excuses to your boss, and you can work from home. I had my children stuffing envelopes and doing name badges for me from a young age, which has given them the work ethic and valuable work experience for finding jobs in the future.'
>
> Elizabeth Cornelius, The Presentation Factor, event management.

Retirement options

The retirement age of 65 is being removed from the workplace, so that people can work longer. This is in line with the pension age being increased, but how realistic is it for 60+-year-olds to find jobs when, despite age discrimination legislation, there is a lot of ageism about?

Being self-employed can prove a better option for older workers, and many will find that their skills, knowledge, expertise and experience are valuable to companies who want to take on staff as and when they need them, with no permanent commitment.

The benefits of being self-employed:

- No more commuting.
- Technology enables you to work anywhere at any time of the day or night.
- You can cut down on your carbon footprint and live a greener lifestyle.
- Quality of life is improved.
- Work life fits personal lifestyle and family commitments.
- Working conditions can be where and how you want them to be.
- No office politics.
- More productive time spent working rather than being involved in chit-chat, meetings or gossip.
- Strong sense of freedom.
- You can do different things – the world's your oyster and you can have three careers!
- You do not necessarily need qualifications.

Some examples of self-employed careers:

Journalism	Public relations consultant
Gardener	Electrician
Plumber	Builder
Roofer	Hairdresser
Teacher	Architect
Financial adviser	Temporary secretary/PA
Event manager	Courier
Beautician	Management consultant
Accountant	Bookkeeper
Counsellor	Complementary therapist
Interior designer	Graphic designer

Sports coach	Market research consultant
Network salesperson	Taxi driver
Auditor	IT consultant
IT engineer	Musician
Actor	Singer
Writer	Artist
Car mechanic	Photographer

No need for a degree

It's not entirely true that you don't need a degree to work for yourself – you may be in an industry where you wouldn't be considered seriously without one – for example in some areas of management consultancy or engineering. You may need a degree to get the relevant experience you need to set up on your own.

However, you do not need qualifications for a wide variety of businesses because it is of no importance to your customers or clients, who are only interested in the service or products you can offer.

Successful entrepreneurs who don't have a degree:

- Bill Gates, CEO, Microsoft
- Steve Jobs, CEO, Apple
- Richard Branson, CEO, Virgin Atlantic
- Lord Alan Sugar, CEO, Amstrad Enterprises
- Sir Philip Green, owner, Arcadia retail group (includes Topshop)
- Jamie Oliver, chef
- Coco Chanel, founder of Chanel
- Simon Cowell, TV producer
- And countless actors, pop stars and sports people

What sort of person are you?

If you like order and security and prefer not to negotiate or organise, self-employment is unlikely to be for you. As a self-employed person you have to do everything, unless you are in a position to appoint people to do some of it for you.

You will have to become a salesperson, selling your service or product to anyone and everyone; run a marketing campaign; handle PR; be your own secretary/PA, bookkeeper and administrator; order the stationery; plan travel arrangements; be an IT expert; and you'll have to buy and make the tea!

If you have been employed for a long time, many of these activities will be handled within the organisation without you giving them a second thought, or without them affecting your own bank balance.

Qualities recommended for self-employment

- Self-discipline.
- Motivation.
- Self-sufficiency.
- Efficiency.
- Self-belief and self-worth.
- Realistic goals.
- Organisational skills.
- Having vision.
- 'Can do' approach.
- Versatility.
- Honesty – towards self.
- Confidence to ask for money.
- Risk-taking.

'If you like order and security and prefer not to negotiate or organise, self-employment is unlikely to be for you. As a self-employed person you have to do everything, unless you are in a position to appoint people to do some of it for you.'

- Ability to work alone (if relevant).
- Pragmatism.
- Resilience – ability to bounce back.
- Tenacity – holding on when times are bad.

Developing the right qualities

The biggest struggle for a self-employed person is often with your own mind. Trying to keep motivated and optimistic when business isn't booming is a real challenge. Bouncing back all the time when there are plenty of setbacks is hard.

Not everyone who is self-employed starts off with the right characteristics, but they develop resilience and many other qualities as time goes on. It can enable people to gain a more philosophical approach to life and a good attitude to problem-solving.

Taking risks

It should be emphasised that risk-taking may be necessary to an extent, but mortgaging your family home on the back of a new business could be a risk too far. It's certainly helpful to be the kind of person who is willing to try new ventures and move into unfamiliar territory out of your comfort zone.

You need to think about lifestyle. If you live alone, will you get lonely? If so is there a chance you could work with other people? Perhaps you can share an office with others in a business hub or centre, or with colleagues. Can you cope with the insecurity of not knowing when your money is going to arrive and that you may have to contend with bad debts?

Case study

'The flexibility of working for yourself is great when you have a family, but I also enjoy the freedom and not having to answer to anyone but myself. I have to meet my own expectations and objectives, not someone else's which suits me as a person. I like having more control over my life and it helps that I'm doing something that I want to do now.

'Of course there is a downside to being self-employed in that you don't get paid for holidays, if you're ill or want some time off. At times it's difficult to keep regular hours because I could make myself available at any time. So I have to set boundaries and be clear about when I work and when I don't.'

Tracey Pennington, Psychotherapeutic Counsellor, Epsom Counselling Service.

The buck stops here

You need to be able to rely on yourself for everything, because that's where the buck stops. The chances are that you will care about your business more wholeheartedly than those who work for you, unless they have a stake in it – perhaps as your partner in business or life.

It's essential that you are confident about what you are doing before you start, that you have researched the market for your industry, and that it is realistic to make a living out of it. Lots of people start up businesses while they are still employed or partially employed so that they have the safety net behind them, and so that they can test the market before taking the plunge of giving up work.

Are your plans credible?

Anyone who watches BBC's *Dragon's Den* will know that there are plenty of budding entrepreneurs who have what they consider to be great ideas that are shot down in flames by the Dragons. This is usually because they are not (a) realistic (b) financially viable or (c) likely to sell at all. Often it is also because the budding 'entrepreneur' has overvalued the business, based on wild estimates.

You need to talk to lots of people about your ideas if you are starting a new venture. This is different if you are in a well-established profession or trade that you know is viable – for example, plumbers know that there is a lot of call for their trade, or if you are training as a driving instructor you can be sure that people are always going to want to learn to drive.

Economic climate

'Many industries have been hit hard by difficult economic times and when jobs are being shed there are more people becoming self-employed. So it is important to assess the economic climate and the impact in your industry.'

Many industries have been hit hard by difficult economic times and when jobs are being shed more people become self-employed. So it is important to assess the economic climate and the impact on your industry. For instance, journalists, beauticians and consultants have to carefully examine the possibilities of going freelance in a marketplace that isn't as favourable as it used to be.

Some careers go through boom times, but they can also spiral downwards too. The Internet has changed the way we live and has had a dramatic effect on some industries such as journalism, because information is so readily available online and it's free. Conversely, the ever-growing digital industry is placing specialists in IT and website design in high demand.

Research the market

Do your research to be sure that the market is there for your industry. Talk to other people who do the same as you and get honest answers, look at the trade media and ask potential clients or customers if they would use you on a self-employed basis.

Better off or not?

For some people, working for themselves may be much better paid than being an employee. The tax system can be slightly more favourable because you can claim expenses, such as running a car, buying stationery, travelling, a proportion of heating and lighting and deterioration of car and computer equipment costs. (See chapter 6.)

There are, however, many pitfalls to being self-employed and it is essential that you look into the detail and consider it very carefully before leaving full-time employment. Some people may not have a choice because they have been made redundant or know that they are too old to get back into their own industry, or it may be common practice to be self-employed in their industry.

In theory, the sky's the limit in terms of earnings, because there's no one dictating what you should be paid. In practice, you have to weigh up the loss of sick pay, holiday pay and pension contributions before making an economic judgement.

Huge growth in self-employment in the 1980s

In the 1980s there was a big rise in the number of people becoming self-employed, particularly among women.

From 1981 to 1991, there was a 78% increase in the number of self-employed women. This was due to a change in social attitudes at that time and government incentives which are no longer in place.

The rise of self-employment in the 1980s also saw:

- An increase in the number of young and formerly unemployed workers.
- Increased diversity of occupations chosen.
- A doubling of the number of people in the service sector.

Based on information from: 'The Distribution of Self-Employment Income in the United Kingdom 1976-1991' by Simon Parker, published in the March 1997 issue of the Economic Journal. Parker is in the Economics Department at the University of Durham. Material used in the analysis came from the Family Expenditure Survey through the Economic and Social Research Council Data Archive.

Since the 1980s the increase in numbers of people becoming self-employed has not increased at the same pace, possibly because of a more difficult economic climate and consequent risk. The government has cracked down on people who work for one company most of the time, including construction workers, forcing them to become employees, rather than contract workers.

Comparison of self-employed from March 1992 to August 2010

March 1992:

Males classified as self-employed: 2,552,000

Females classified as self-employed: 899,000

August 2010:

Males classified as self-employed: 2,824,000

Females: 1,148,000

Increase in eight years:

Men: 272,000

Women: 249,000

Source: UK Statistics Authority website: www.statisticsauthority.gov.uk or www.statistics.gov.uk

Full-time, part-time and temporary workers											United Kingdom (thousands) seasonally adjusted
	All in employment					Total in employment		Employees		Self-employed	
	Total 1	Employees 1	Self employed	Unpaid family workers	Government supported training & employment programmes	Full-time	Part-time	Full-time	Part-time	Full-time	Part-time	Workers with second jobs
150	1	2	3	4	5	6	7	8	9	10	11	12
All Persons	MGRZ	MGRN	MGRQ	MGRT	MGRW	YCBE	YCBH	YCBK	YCBN	YCBQ	YCBT	YCBW
Jun-Aug 2008	29,429	25,422	3,810	92	105	21,923	7,506	18,969	6,453	2,901	910	1,114
Jun-Aug 2009	28,917	24,842	3,880	87	108	21,312	7,605	18,343	6,499	2,912	968	1,129
Sep-Nov 2009	28,905	24,839	3,879	79	108	21,202	7,703	18,267	6,572	2,888	991	1,124
Dec-Feb 2010	28,843	24,761	3,873	89	120	21,163	7,681	18,232	6,529	2,884	989	1,086
Mar-May 2010	28,980	24,837	3,929	86	128	21,161	7,819	18,203	6,634	2,905	1,023	1,133
Jun-Aug 2010	29,158	24,943	3,972	110	134	21,196	7,962	18,186	6,757	2,948	1,023	1,113
Male	MGSA	MGRO	MGRR	MGRU	MGRX	YCBF	YCBI	YCBL	YCBO	YCBR	YCBU	YCBX
Jun-Aug 2008	15,883	13,021	2,766	32	65	14,052	1,831	11,638	1,383	2,381	385	450
Jun-Aug 2009	15,441	12,584	2,761	36	60	13,576	1,865	11,173	1,410	2,366	395	489
Sep-Nov 2009	15,395	12,560	2,744	34	57	13,520	1,874	11,151	1,409	2,343	401	481
Dec-Feb 2010	15,368	12,531	2,736	39	62	13,481	1,887	11,125	1,406	2,329	407	459
Mar-May 2010	15,483	12,604	2,763	40	76	13,534	1,949	11,161	1,443	2,342	421	476
Jun-Aug 2010	15,615	12,662	2,824	46	84	13,585	2,030	11,161	1,501	2,385	439	458
Female	MGSB	MGRP	MGRS	MGRV	MGRY	YCBG	YCBJ	YCBM	YCBP	YCBS	YCBV	YCBY
Jun-Aug 2008	13,545	12,401	1,045	59	40	7,871	5,674	7,332	5,069	520	524	664
Jun-Aug 2009	13,477	12,258	1,119	51	48	7,737	5,740	7,169	5,089	545	574	640
Sep-Nov 2009	13,510	12,278	1,135	45	51	7,682	5,829	7,116	5,163	545	590	643
Dec-Feb 2010	13,476	12,230	1,137	51	58	7,682	5,794	7,107	5,123	555	582	626
Mar-May 2010	13,497	12,233	1,166	46	53	7,627	5,870	7,042	5,191	564	602	656
Jun-Aug 2010	13,543	12,281	1,148	65	50	7,611	5,932	7,025	5,256	564	584	654

Summing Up

The world is your oyster when you are self-employed. You can have a 'portfolio' career, doing three or four different things, or specialise in one. You can suit yourself when you work and you have control over your destiny with the option to earn much more money than as an employee. But it isn't easy because you are responsible for everything and have to be able to handle all aspects of running a business. It can also be risky, stressful and worrying, so you need to think carefully about whether you are cut out to take the risk of not having a guaranteed salary each month.

Chapter Two

Planning Your Self-employed Career

Think very carefully before you embark on a self-employed career, particularly if you are giving up a job to do so. In the 1980s, in the UK, many people started working as self-employed because there was plenty of work around and the economy was in good shape. That is not the case at the time of writing and it is a much more risky business.

There are many good sides to being self-employed, principally the facts that you are in charge of yourself and do not have a direct boss, and that you can fit your lifestyle around your work. The rewards and benefits must also be offset by realism as working for yourself can be enormously challenging.

Few businesses make a good profit in the first year though, so it is important to have start-up funds or another source of income, either your own or your partner's.

'The rewards and benefits must also be offset by realism as working for yourself can be enormously challenging.'

Responsibility to yourself

You do not have the comfort of a company who will pay you when you get sick, or that gives you holiday pay and other benefits such as a pension, National Insurance contributions and a bonus.

It is in your interests to keep yourself healthy, because if you can't work, you can't earn. Spending too long at the computer, doing heavy labour, working every hour that you possibly can, may make you more susceptible to illness, RSI and back pain, eye strain and stress. You are much more indispensable as a self-employed worker and therefore you need to look after yourself.

Take advantage of the freedom you have to stop when you like, go for a walk, sit in the garden and relax. It's important to draw boundaries about when you do and don't work. Some people who work at home do not ever work on weekends. Those who do may choose to have a day off in the week.

Are you suited to self-employment? Checklist

- [ ] Are you prepared to put in plenty of time and effort to get your business off the ground?
- [ ] Can you cope with financial insecurity and making sacrifices if necessary?
- [ ] Do you have financial back-up – either from a partner, another regular income or savings?
- [ ] Does your family or partner support your decision to become self-employed?
- [ ] Can you cope with working alone, not as part of a team?
- [ ] Are you an organised person, who can manage all aspects of the business efficiently?
- [ ] Do you have entrepreneurial spirit – are you an ideas person who doesn't rely on others in the workplace?
- [ ] Are you capable of, and good at, managing staff if you need to?

'People prefer to do business with people they like who seem confident and friendly. If you come over as anxious and depressed, the chances are your business won't do well.'

A sense of security

Easing into self-employment can give you that essential sense of security that enables you to feel confident about starting up a new business. Just having two days a week working somewhere doing something else can take away the worry about finances and provide the security required for you to give your best to the new business.

As perception is half the battle, you will be a more effective self-employed person if you don't spend your whole life worrying about it. People prefer to do business with people they like, who seem confident and friendly. If you come over as anxious and depressed, the chances are your business won't do well.

Need2Know

Jack of all trades

On top of being responsible for every penny you earn and how you earn it, you have to find solutions to why your PC is playing up, pay for your own car, buy yourself a new printer, check there is enough stationery, keep an eye on the bank account, handle your accounts and manage cash flow.

If you're working at home and the computer hard drive crashes, you run out of stationery, or you need a new desk, you have to take time out of your day to deal with it, and sometimes these niggling things can seriously impede upon your working time.

If you employ staff, you may get embroiled in dealing with them, delegating work to them, ensuring they are doing what they should, having meetings, discussing issues that they have and much more. Once you have employees you automatically have more financial responsibilities and can no longer run the business just to suit yourself.

The advent of the Internet and the way it has revolutionised the office, can at times seem to be a blessing in disguise. Before you even get down to doing your core work you have to check your emails. Whether you are employed or self-employed, dealing with emails can take up a good part of each day, as it's like having a huge influx of post to deal with.

You will also have to do the marketing – you may be an expert in your field but you will have to learn to sell, sell, sell, and be knowledgeable about and able to handle PR, advertising, websites, exhibitions and other promotional areas, or spend time outsourcing them.

And that's before you've started doing the work that you actually do!

Qualities a self-employed person needs:

- Confidence – to be in business and persuade others of the viability.
- Enthusiasm – to believe in yourself and what you are doing.
- Determination – to succeed despite the odds.
- Self-reliance – you may be the only person you can count on.

- Financial sense – to manage finances.
- Comfortable with talking finance – to negotiate fees/costs and ensure prompt payment.
- The ability to develop strategies to help you overcome problems.
- A 'can do' attitude – you and you alone have to do it.
- Good judgement – you make the main decisions.
- Tenacity to keep going when times are tough.
- Commitment – not to give up when things go wrong.
- Energy – to cope with the ups and downs.
- Forthrightness – to approach people about work and sell.
- Humility – to do any job that needs doing.
- Discipline – to work hard, but not to become a workaholic.
- Focus – to be able to see what needs doing and how to do it.
- Vision – to see where the business is going, particularly in tough times.
- Oodles of common sense – not to make rash and dangerous decisions.

Useful attributes

You may be an excellent lawyer, but can you run your own business? It goes without saying that you should be good at what you set out to do, but you must be business savvy as well. It's a tough world out there and unless you can stand up to people and keep your feet on the ground, you could come unstuck. Most companies fail in their first year for a variety of reasons (see chapter 7, Coping With the Pitfalls).

'It goes without saying that you should be good at what you set out to do, but you must be business savvy as well. It's a tough world out there and unless you can stand up to people and keep your feet on the ground you could come unstuck.'

Start-up essentials

Do your research:

- You need to know and understand the market for your services or products.

- Who will your competitors be? If they are established companies, look them up on the Web, find out what marketing they do, and how well they do.

- Find out who you will be able to work with or for and where your own market will be. Talk to potential clients/customers.

- If the market is well-established, investigate it as if you were a customer/client.

- Ask questions of everyone you know in the same field of business.

- If you are making a product, check out all the legal implications.

- Find out what costs are involved and what profit you should expect to make.

- You must be sure of how to bring your product/services to market.

- What makes you different? What is your USP (unique selling point)?

What will you do?

For many people there is an obvious path to go down, which isn't new to them. If you are already a teacher, a journalist, an accountant, a gardener, a builder or have expertise in computers, carpentry or design, you may know the market and start up as a self-employed person with knowledge and experience.

Plenty of people decide to start up a new business altogether because of a brainwave, an opportunity that has arisen or where they feel there is a gap in the market. Alternatively, you may choose to retrain in something completely different, such as a counsellor, a teacher, a complementary therapist, or a driving instructor, most of which you can do while holding down a job as well.

It's quite common for self-employed people to have what's known as a portfolio career, which means that you do several different things. This can make your work very interesting and it also means that if one area of business is not doing well, you have others to fall back on.

Case study

'I like the control and flexibility that being self-employed brings. Because I have variety in the types of yoga classes I teach, as well as accountancy, it keeps me fresh and enthusiastic. There can be a downside to working for yourself in that it can be very volatile, but I have regular lessons and fixed contracts which helps a lot.

'I don't earn as much as when I was involved in insolvency, but I can look back at that time and realise that I was very stressed and overworked. I was caught in a spiral that I found difficult to extricate myself from. That kind of work is very money-driven, but it felt like I was preying on the misfortunes of others. Now I am teaching yoga to adults and children with learning difficulties which is much more rewarding.

'I feel that I have a sense of pride in working for myself, in that I am seeing the fruits of my own labour.'

Richard Kravetz, accountant and yoga teacher, Yoga for Health

---

Choosing a career

Services

There are many types of service you can provide to people drawing on your skills, your knowledge, something you feel is needed in your area, or something you know you will love doing. You may see a gap in the market and decide to fill it, or think that you can do a better job than others already doing it. There are many choices including:

Computer consultancy or repairs, advertising, public relations, complementary therapies, teaching English as a foreign language, management consultancy, making cakes, bookkeeping, training or coaching, gardening, cleaning, car repairs, plumbing, translation, event management, accountancy, beauty treatments, chauffeuring, and so on.

Products

Selling products that you may import or source in the UK, or make yourself. Increasingly these are sold over the Internet, but may be sold in a shop, by telephone and/or on the Internet.

Franchise

Starting up your own business using a recognised brand.

Multilevel marketing

Selling products from one manufacturer by developing tiers of sales people below you.

Direct selling

Plenty of opportunities for working at home, including party plans, through established companies.

Opportunities for women

A growing number of women are 'rebelling' against the traditional 9-5 working day so that they can spend more time with their family while still having a career, according to a survey conducted by Avon and parenting website, Netmums.com. It found that one in eight are looking for a better work/life balance, often by starting their own business.

The survey of 2,200 women found that over two-thirds would consider working longer hours if they could spend more time with their families, something that is possible with self-employment.

Siobhan Freegard, co-founder of Netmums.com, said: 'Many mums want to work for both the financial freedom and sense of achievement they get from having a successful livelihood, but not to the detriment of their children.

'We hear every day from mums who are finding it stressful and frustrating trying to get a work/life balance due to the lack of flexible working and part-time jobs.'

Netmums is a brilliant resource for mothers who need to work and want to find opportunities (see help list). It has long lists of companies involved in:

- Direct selling opportunities, one of the most common and longest established being Avon.
- Franchise opportunities.
- Local directories of selling opportunities in your area.

It also gives information on other ways of making money such as:

- Fostering.
- Childminding.
- Selling real nappies.

For an excellent list of opportunities go to: http://www.netmums.com/working/Working_from_home.430/

Research the market

Services

If you are providing a service that you have a lot of knowledge about, you are likely to know the market. Look at the competitors, look at what they charge and try to find out how successful they are.

Providing services makes you very flexible as you can change what you offer at any time. For instance, if you are good at maintaining computers you may start a business servicing and fixing them. You may, in your spare time, learn how to design a website and then you can add this as another service.

The other advantage is that you do not have to buy or store products, meaning that you have less of a cash outlay and low overheads.

However, time is money and you can only earn as much as you have time to do, but if you do become successful you can pay others to help you or you can sub-contract. Often you can employ other self-employed people without having to get involved in PAYE.

Getting business

In certain industries such as copywriting, PR, advertising, event management, design and consultancy, a lot of time is spent getting a sale. Much of your work is speculative and you can find yourself working hard to try and get business, only to find that someone else has clinched the deal.

It also happens a lot that clients change their minds before they commit money, and your speculative work that has taken a lot of time and effort, may be consigned to the bin. This is very frustrating for people in these industries and does not currently seem to have a resolution, particularly as times are harder and it is a buyer's market.

Contracts

In theory, small businesses should have signed contracts to agree terms – how much they will be paid and how much notice is required. In practice this doesn't always happen, but it is a necessary protection to ensure that clients don't default on payments.

Always invoice on time and lay down rules about length of payment. In some businesses it is possible to get part-payment up front, which is obviously very satisfactory. Otherwise put on your invoice 'Payment terms: 30 days' – this is long enough to wait for payment, but there are some UK companies who have a policy of paying after 60 days or even more. Publishers often pay journalists on publication, which can mean waiting months for payment and can seriously affect cash flow.

In the case of tradesmen it is normal practice for a builder or decorator to be paid as soon as the job is finished, or in part-payment throughout the job. They may need to buy materials and will normally ask for stage payments.

'Always invoice on time and lay down rules about length of payment. In some businesses it is possible to get part-payment up front which is obviously very satisfactory.'

Case study

'I became self-employed because of the situation in my previous job which had changed and meant that I was going to have to work shifts. Freedom is the first thing that comes to mind, but of course you aren't completely free to do as you like because you have customers that you have to answer to. They expect you to arrive at a regular time each week, but the customer definitely doesn't take the place of a boss. There's no one actually telling you what to do.

'The main problem for me is the weather which dictates when I can work. In a harsh winter I can lose about three months, because the jobs that people would have asked me to do in January are put off if there's snow on the ground for a long time. By the end of the winter they no longer want those particular jobs doing.

'I would have found it very worrying not having a regular salary if the children had still been dependent on us, but now it's easier. I am definitely pleased that I made the break when I did.'

Doug Clark, contract and private gardener.

Products

Selling products means that you have the potential to make lots of profit, because you can sell as many as you have orders for, within reason and provided you have enough to sell. Profit doesn't depend on how much time you spend working, although the busier you are the more time is taken up in administration and may require extra staff or outsourcing.

Be sure of your target market and try not to pay for stock until you have guaranteed sales or you could end up out of pocket. Consider the best ways of selling – on the Internet you might need a dedicated website, or you may be able to sell through eBay. Perhaps you can sell locally with ads in papers and shop windows. You may want to sell direct to retail outlets, in which case talk to some of them before you commit to the products.

One of the key advantages of selling products as opposed to services, is that you usually get paid up front for them, ensuring that you don't part with any goods until you have received the money.

E-commerce is big business now and needs to be factored in when you are having your website designed. Web designers are well aware of how to set up e-commerce and can provide you with the different options to make your site easy to use and easy to purchase from. It is essential that it is simple and easy for the customer and accepting PayPal and credit and debit cards are essential.

Franchises

There are many very successful franchises in the UK, some of which are quite large, such as pizza outlets, printing and design bureaux, children's parties and yoga classes. The advantages of joining up with a well-established franchise is that there is plenty of help and information, as well as marketing systems and available stock. The business model is well defined and it may be better recognised by banks if you are hoping to borrow money.

Franchises can require considerable outlay initially on an annual basis and must not be considered lightly. You need to know in detail what the likely returns are to see if it is a viable proposition for you. As they are tried and tested there's every chance that you can make them succeed, but consider your position carefully.

Where they are located is important – you won't do so well if there are three other photocopying bureaux in the vicinity.

There are numerous types of franchises (see www.franchisesales.co.uk):

- Dating agencies.
- Ice creams.
- Automotive parts.
- Organic vegetables.
- Computer repairs.
- Home maintenance.
- Car valeting.
- Pet grooming.
- Health supplements.
- Children's parties.
- Stationery.
- And much, much more.

Be very careful about franchises you haven't heard of, that no one else has heard of and that are requesting large sums of money. You need to visit other people operating the franchise and see if they are genuinely making money out of it. Take advice, talk to Business Link, (see help list) about it, and do your research well.

Once you have a franchise, be sure that they stick to their own rules and that you keep a watchful eye on what the owners are doing, examine their accounts and find out about their marketing and support on a regular basis.

Bear in mind that the first money you earn is simply going towards repaying the cost of the franchise.

For more information on franchises:

www.british-franchise.org/ or www.whichfranchise.com/

www.netmums.org.uk/

Multilevel marketing

This kind of opportunity often gets a bad press and some people steer clear of them. The facts are that some people do well out of it and make a good living, and others can either lose money or make very little. It probably depends on your personality.

You might have to pay a fee to start up which may be a reasonable figure, but if you are paying out you need to do the same careful research you would do for a franchise. You are heavily encouraged to create a team of distributors beneath you, so that every time they make a sale you get commission.

You must be the kind of person who is willing to sell to everyone you know, including your family and friends, because you will be encouraged to do so. You are looking for repeat business so you need to maintain a relationship with them and hope to keep selling to them.

It is usually expected that you will co-opt other distributors beneath you who you have to motivate to sell. This is the way that some people make a lot of money, because they have so much commission coming in from the tier of people below them and in turn those beneath them, and so on.

This kind of marketing emanated from the US, so be aware that there are regular meetings which often sound rather evangelical and where people are awarded for their sales figures.

It costs nothing to go to a meeting and see for yourself, but again, do your research and talk to other distributors before signing up. Be careful not to buy too much stock without guaranteed sales.

Be prepared

The best way to start up on your own is to have clients and customers from the outset. If you have both contacts and contracts lined up, it will start you off. Similarly, you may stay in part-time employment or continue in a line of work that is flexible while you are setting up your business.

This is a much safer way of doing things. Of course you won't have this luxury if you are made redundant and didn't have time to prepare. Although plenty of people try something different; if you are in this situation, you might find it easier to go with what you already know.

Plenty of people leave a job and keep the company as a client which means that they have guaranteed work straightaway, but you no longer have a job and nothing is certain. People can change their minds about offering you work, and decide not to go ahead, quite often for reasons that are to do with them and not you. You need to be sure that you have work to start off with, unless you have sufficient funds.

'The best way to start up on your own is to have clients and customers from the outset. If you have both contacts and contracts lined up it will start you off.'

Summing Up

It may be obvious to you what you will do as a self-employed person – if you have a trade or a profession you may want to set up on your own. Alternatively, your circumstances may dictate that you need to be self-employed, but you don't know what to do, or maybe you need to earn extra money and think that starting a business as well as working part-time or full-time is the way to go. If you have been made redundant and cannot find a job, or have young children and need to be at home to care for them when they aren't at school, it presents a viable option.

There are lots of possibilities when you look around as there are many businesses that lend themselves to self-employment, and many other companies who require self-employed people to work for them.

Chapter Three

Financing Your Business

The global economic crisis and the squeeze on British banks changed the landscape for borrowing in the UK and worldwide. It is much more difficult to get funding for a business now from a bank, whereas in the 1980s banks were handing out money quite liberally. This is probably a good thing because so many people borrowed money for ventures that didn't work and ended up with a lot of debt.

The other options are:

- Use redundancy payment.
- Use your own savings.
- Ask a family member to back you.
- Increase the mortgage on your house (but this could be risky).
- Go into business with a partner who can invest.

For a lot of people starting up, there is no need to obtain finance and in some cases, where they are providing a service on a freelance basis, they would be unlikely to attract any funding.

Government help

Government cuts and changes make it impossible to reliably indicate exactly what government or local government funding is available to small businesses.

At the time of writing, the government is planning to introduce a new Enterprise Allowance Scheme, but it seems that this is only available to unemployed people and not to everyone wishing to start a new business.

'Government cuts and changes make it impossible to reliably indicate exactly what government or local government funding is available to small businesses.'

This means that anyone wishing to set up a new business and receive the allowance may have to register as unemployed, but you would have to check how long you have to be unemployed to qualify for the scheme. It is, however, worth investigating.

There are also a number of regional enterprise schemes, but these are dealt with on a local basis and vary according to where you are.

BIS is the government's Department for Business Innovation and Skills that used to be the Department of Trade and Industry (DTI), (see help list). They provide information about funding on their website: www.bsi.gov.uk.

The department has streamlined the Solutions for Business support for businesses through Business Link: www.businesslink.gov.uk and Regional Development Agencies (RDAs) and Local Authorities are also partners in delivering this support.

Business Link

Business Link is the first place to go to find out how you can get funding. They have access to a number of organisations throughout the UK that provide finance to business, and can also put you in touch with a programme called Access to Finance that, for a small fee, helps you to understand where you can access money.

They will also be able to advise on the viability of getting a bank loan, although banks have become notoriously difficult to get funding from since the credit crunch in the late noughties.

Sources of finance

- Grants and awards – operated by various organisations and companies, often on a regional level. Advice from Business Link.

- Business Angels – individuals or small companies who make a living out of lending money to small businesses. Look at Angel News, http://www.angelnews.co.uk, a website that puts entrepreneurs in touch with investors and provides news and information.

'Starting up a business can be risky. It is much better if you do not need to borrow any money and live within the income that your business generates, so that you do not get into debt. Debt free is best.'

Richard Kravetz, accountant and yoga teacher.

- Venture capital – usually on a big scale, but there is plenty of lending still going on and foreign investment for innovations, particularly on environmental projects.

- Business Link can help with all aspects of accessing finance and should be the first port of call when you need to get investment. Call the national number in the help list and you will be directed to your local branch. They have considerable information about all aspects of setting up in business and because they are a government-funded operation, they aren't trying to sell you products.

They also give advice on their website: www.businesslink.gov.uk, including how to write a business plan.

Dragon's Den

Most people requiring money as a start-up will look to their family, their own money, remortgage their property or go to Dragon's Den – this is a realistic proposition because if you have a brilliant idea there are Dragon's Den online and on TV possibilities. Watch the programme first before pitching up with a wild idea! Some people win with fantastic inventions, but others have found a viable and different business proposition that stacks up financially.

Business plan

There are various reasons for writing a business plan:

- Seeking finance, loan or big investment.

- For lease commitment on a building – can you realistically afford it?

- It makes good business sense.

Some people advocate writing a business plan so that you can be focused on making your business run according to plan. In reality, some people cannot forecast business because it depends on retaining clients or market forces which are out of their control.

'Some people advocate writing a business plan so that you can be focused on making your business run according to plan. In reality, some people cannot forecast business because it depends on retaining clients or market forces which are out of their control.'

Writing a business plan

There are detailed instructions as to how to write a business plan on Business Link's website, and they show you samples from a variety of industries, which are helpful to anyone starting up. It shows the correct format and emphasises what are the most important aspects when creating a business plan.

The business plan must include a number of essential details:

- Description of the business, the target market.
- Your background, your business idea and why you have decided to set it up.
- Goals of the business and why it is likely to succeed.
- Requirements in terms of staff, equipment, etc.
- Potential problems you might encounter – how to deal with these.
- Competition in the market place, potential or gaps in the market.
- Marketing plan, including advertising and PR.
- Budgeting and managing company growth.
- Financial: capital equipment and supply list, balance sheet, income statement and cash flow analysis, sales and expense forecast.

Summing Up

In difficult financial times it can be hard to raise finance for a small business, but there are always opportunities for someone with a good commercial idea. Business Link is very helpful at pointing small businesses in the direction of finance and it is well worth getting in touch with them. If you do make a formal application for finance you will need to write a business plan, and there is plenty of advice on this from Business Link as well. It makes good sense to start a business without borrowing any money, so if you have a nest egg or someone in the family who can provide investment, that's even better.

Chapter Four

Where Will You Work?

Choosing the right place to work is an essential part of planning your self-employed career. There are several options:

- Using space in your own home – a bedroom, a study, a garage or shed that you can convert.

- Using space in someone else's home – either paying for it or using it for free.

- Renting office space in a business centre or business hub.

- Renting an office.

- Buying office space.

- Hot desking.

- Co-working.

We will look at each of these options in turn during this chapter.

There are many factors that you need to take into consideration such as: how much space you need; whether or not clients/customers will visit you; whether you can afford to pay rent; if it is suitable to work at home; if you have the freedom to be out at the office – for instance, if you are working around children you may prefer to be at hand, at home.

In some cases, you don't need an office, shop or other premises, as you work at other sites – for instance, a tennis coach, a gardener, or an actress will be working away from home.

All office expenses can be written off against tax and that includes your rental and use of any services such as secretarial, telephone answering, photocopies, or bookkeeping.

You will be able to claim the conversion of a room for office purposes against tax, plus any equipment you require to set up your home workspace. You can claim a small proportion of your utility bills too and any building work you pay for to create business space can also be offset.

Things to consider

Insurance

Types of insurance you may need:

- Public liability insurance if you are working with members of the public, or there is any chance of people being at risk – in a car workshop, a dance studio, or if you are a builder – you are likely to need this.

- Critical illness cover, insurance against loss of earnings due to illness. This can be called Critical Illness Cover, Income Protection Insurance, Personal Accident and Sickness Insurance. Shop around for competitive quotes.

- Contents/buildings insurance of goods, premises or expensive equipment.

Health and safety

Be aware of all of your obligations if you have a lot of visitors or staff.

Outsourcing

You do not need to employ people to get the help you need. There are virtual PA companies, as well as individuals you might know, who can work for you as and when they can. If you like to sound like you have a receptionist you can pay for office answering services, so that someone takes messages for you.

Working from home

The advantages:

- No rent to pay.
- No travelling required to work.
- You can be flexible about hours you work.
- You can run your work life around your family commitments.
- Everything is in one place.
- You can save money on lunches, parking, fares and other extras.
- You have the opportunity for a quiet environment.
- You can have the windows open or closed, the radio on or off, you can sit in the garden when you need to read documents – the world is your oyster.

The disadvantages:

- No separation between work and leisure.
- If you have young children you may not get peace and quiet.
- You can feel lonely and miss having people around you.
- It may encourage you to work all hours and become a workaholic.
- You may find yourself doing other things and not working – gardening, household chores, chatting on the phone.
- Sometimes, other people don't recognise that you are working because you are at home.

Most people have an idea as to whether or not they would like to work from home. You may already have a room in mind which is suitable for turning into an office, or you may want to convert a garage or shed to become an office.

If you do not already have substantial funds to start your business, it isn't wise to spend a lot of money on an elaborate conversion at the outset. Some people start working in the spare bedroom and create purpose-built office space when they become more successful and need more space.

'Some people start working in the spare bedroom and create purpose-built office space when they become more successful and need more space.'

You will be able to claim the conversion of a room for office purposes against tax, plus any equipment you require to set up your home workspace. You can claim a small proportion of your utility bills too and any building work you pay for to create business space can also be offset. Either consult an accountant about this, or check directly with the tax office, who are very helpful.

Some people find that working at home is not for them. They may not feel professional, or they may get lonely and need the buzz of a working environment and/or like-minded people to work alongside. For many, particularly mothers, it can be an excellent solution.

Case study

'Over 20 years ago I became involved in selling insurance for which you had to be self-employed. It has become a way of life now, but it can be a double-edged sword because you need to be disciplined to work for yourself and it can be lonely, particularly if you are living alone.

'Although I sometimes think about becoming employed again I am probably unemployable now because I don't have the right mindset. Having to answer to someone else would be difficult, but there is a danger when you work for yourself that you become so used to making decisions that you are convinced you are right, and you cannot be right all the time.

'Sometimes I crave the idea of turning up at work, doing a job well and getting paid at the end of the month, without the pressure of having to bring the work in. It could be good to have a team to work with so that you come to conclusions quicker and in a more structured way. But doing what other people want you to do doesn't really suit me, and even though it might be nice to have the banter of lots of colleagues it could be distracting.

'Training to be a TEFL teacher has added another dimension to my life and made me enjoy my other work more too. Teaching English obviously involves working with other people so it enables me to have a better balance. My current aim is to move into serviced offices with a couple of colleagues so that I have the opportunity to be around others as and when it suits me.'

Giles Sanger, Independent Financial Adviser, GSS Financial Planning, and teacher of English as a foreign language.

Working from someone else's home

It may be that your parents have a large house and would be happy to let you use one of the rooms. This may mean that you do not have to pay rent or you may agree to pay a nominal sum to provide them with an income. You might have other family members who have a spare room in their house or flat that you could use, or others you know who will rent rooms out.

Advantages:

- Could be free or cheap.
- You are getting out of your own house.
- It might prove good company for your parents or other family members.
- You can separate home and office.

Disadvantages:

- You may feel obliged to spend time with your parents/relatives instead of working.
- You may not feel independent.
- It isn't very sociable and is not a working environment.
- You cannot control the environment if it is disturbing you.

Business centres and hubs

Since the 1980s, the rise in sole traders and small businesses resulted in the development of serviced offices in which business people rent a room in a centre where certain services are included, and with additional services if required.

A great option for some who:

- Don't want to work from home.
- Need to look professional and have clients visit them.
- Want to have other businesses around them.

'Since the 1980s, the rise in sole traders and small businesses resulted in the development of serviced offices in which business people rent a room in a centre where certain services are included, and with additional services if required.'

- Like to keep business separate from personal life.
- Need facilities, such as phone answering, PA and clerical services, photocopier and fax.
- Need a reception for packages and other deliveries.

Included in the rent may be:

- Office furniture and telephone.
- Telephone answering.
- Reception services.
- Wireless network/broadband facility.
- Car parking.
- Cleaning.
- Insurance and maintenance of the building.
- Council taxes, utility bills.
- Security.

Additional services may include:

- Board room or meeting room.
- Photocopier and faxes.
- Secretarial services.
- Business advice, bookkeeping, accountancy.
- IT support.

There are few disadvantages to the serviced office, business centre or hub, except that the rental can be quite high. If your business can afford it, it's a great option, but rent has to be paid monthly so you need to have a steady income.

The best way to find business centres, hubs or serviced offices (all the same thing) is to look on the Internet, in the local Yellow Pages or Thomson Directory, or buy a local paper and look at the adverts.

Virtual offices

You don't actually rent a place to work from but you want to look professional with a business address and a receptionist answering the phone for you.

The 'virtual office' offers:

- Business address.
- Telephone number/answering/voicemail.
- Receptionist – post and parcel collection.
- Meeting room.

Co-working

All the same facilities as a serviced office, but you share with other independents and freelancers, and this can be synergistic. It can enable you to do business with your new colleagues, work together and be in a supportive environment rather than being at home. If you don't have a dedicated room, this can be reasonably priced, and is particularly common in large cities like London.

Hot desking

If you don't need office space most of the time, but sometimes need the facilities offered by a professional working environment, hot desking can be the answer. You rent a desk literally for the hour, the day or the week and can take advantage of PA/secretarial and other services offered by the centre.

Business club

Similarly, there are often meeting rooms available on the same basis in business clubs, of which there are several in major cities. Membership entitles you to use facilities as and when you need them, which can be particularly useful if you need to meet clients or staff but don't have premises. Clubs have wireless networks and drinks and food may be available.

Renting self-contained space

If you need a lot of space and have several people working with you, you can rent a self-contained office, which could work out to be less expensive than renting individual rooms in a business centre.

You may have several reasons for needing your own space. It might be suitable if you have a lot of visitors, or if you need specialised space – for instance, garage space, warehousing, workshop, or for a beauty salon.

What to look for:

- How long you are tied into renting premises for.
- The lease period, if you have one, which should be checked by a legal advisor.
- What the notice period is.
- That you have guaranteed income to cover this period.
- You are responsible for everything – insurances, heat and lighting bills, and even council tax.
- Check the location for transport convenience.
- Be sure the neighbourhood is somewhere you are happy to be, or invite people to.

Buying property

For a viable company, partnership or even a sole trader, buying a property to work in can be very worthwhile. As opposed to renting, you are investing in your business, rather than paying money out each month with no return.

You may want to purchase a property to work in for the same reasons as anyone would like to rent independent space, but also because it makes financial sense. It could be a more worthwhile investment than a self-employed private pension.

Things to watch

- Capital gains tax implications – if it is a second property.
- You need guaranteed income to pay the mortgage, unless you can make a cash purchase.
- You will be fully responsible for maintenance, council tax, utility bills.
- Transport links, reasonable location and room to park cars.

PO Box

For between £100 and £200 you can have a PO Box address which enables you to look professional, without using your home address. It also keeps your home address anonymous, which can be important in some businesses. The postman will deliver the mail to your house just as normal.

Case study

Gavin Eddy went to live in Somerset after leaving his job as an investment banker in London. 'My initial intention was to focus on angel investment for businesses in the south-west.' It didn't take Gavin long to decide that if he were investing in companies they would be easier to manage if they were all in one workspace.

'In looking at lots of companies for investment, I discovered that the options for small business workspace were very limited. I thought that as well as offering mentoring, networking, advice and potentially investment to businesses, I could provide flexible and affordable workspace. It was almost by accident that I found out that there was existing demand.

'Thanks to developments in communications and IT infrastructure, many companies no longer need to be based in big cities, but they want workspace options that are consistent with their business aspirations. Work hubs in town centres provide viable alternatives to small high growth businesses to stay local and reduce their overheads and carbon footprint.'

Gavin set up Forward Space which employs five people and provides workspace to small businesses from sole traders to six or seven staff with office services and management on site, in converted listed buildings or those with character – including a former school, a tannery and a shirt and collar factory. The target market for Forward Space is start-ups and emerging companies in their first five years. The company provides business advice, mentoring and support as required, and Gavin will even assist with identifying potential investors.

As well as studios and offices, there are facilities for hot desking (when someone wants office space for just a couple of hours) and co-working, where you share an open-plan office and just pay for the time you use. Each building has its own manager (the 'host') who organises a programme of events including peer to peer talks, presentations and social networking. IT support and virtual PAs are outsourced.

Gavin Eddy, Managing Director, Forward Space

'Thanks to developments in communications and IT infrastructure, many companies no longer need to be based in big cities, but they want workspace options that are consistent with their business aspirations.'

Gavin Eddy, Forward Space.

Summing Up

Choosing where to work is very important when planning your new business. If you are setting up completely alone, home may be the best choice, because it's rent-free and very convenient if you are running your work around your family. There are plenty of options when it comes to office space too. If you need a lot of space you may want to rent an office to accommodate your business, or move into a business centre or serviced offices where everything is provided. It's important that where you are located is suitable for your business, within your budget, and provides contact with others if you want that.

Chapter Five

What Your
Business Needs

It's likely that you will have an initial outlay on equipment and furniture if you are setting up a business from scratch. You may not have an office but you might need specific equipment – workmen's tools, a massage couch, sound equipment, Apple Macs, or kitting out a workshop or garage.

If you are renting space it is quite common for furniture to be included, which can be helpful. You may already own the equipment you need which helps to keep start-up costs to a minimum, but for those that have to set up a new office there are a lot of things to consider.

Office furniture

If you are working from home you could use a suitable table that you can set up as your desk. Make sure that a desk is up to 29 inches (73cm) from the ground, particularly if you are using a computer, so that you don't get RSI (repetitive strain injury) from using the keyboard. You need plenty of space on the desk and if possible your papers, phone and bits and pieces should be on a side desk, so it's not too cluttered.

Computer use is one of the worst problems for office workers, causing a huge increase in the numbers of people with back pain. You should not use laptops on your lap (despite the name), but on a desk of the recommended height or you may notice neck and shoulder pain becoming a side effect.

Sitting comfortably

It's important not to grab a dining room chair and work on it. Try to make sure you have a proper office chair – one that is adjustable and that supports your back. Your legs should fit properly under the desk and it is better to have your feet flat on the floor, and sit straight in front of the desk, not at an angle.

Some people like kneeling stools for working at computers, as they make you sit as if you're riding a horse with your back straight. In this case you can't have your feet on the ground, but you could alternate with a standard office chair.

If you remind yourself to get up every 20 minutes it will give your back some relief, and try not to lean into the computer (everyone does this) but stay back from it. Hands-free phones enable you to talk without holding a handset to your ear. The tendency when working is to cradle it in your neck and end up with pain and stiffness.

If your eyes hurt when you're using a computer, it may mean that you need prescription glasses to wear when working.

'You can run a virtual office at home or even on the move. Mobile phones and laptops have revolutionised the workplace so that you can be in touch by email, or by phone wherever you are and at any time.'

Technology

Technology has made it far easier to work for yourself or from home. You can run a virtual office at home or even on the move. Mobile phones and laptops have revolutionised the workplace so that you can be in touch by email or by phone wherever you are and at any time. This, of course, has disadvantages too, because you have no protection from people contacting you at all hours.

The things you take for granted in an office – telephones, computers, broadband, and all the software, have to be organised by you. This is great if you are IT savvy, but if you're not, it can be mind-boggling.

Landlines

Some people still want to have a landline for business, either because it seems more appropriate to the business they are in, or because they don't relish having a mobile on their ear for hours on end. Handsets can be very cheap either online or at stores like Argos, and you can shop around for deals.

BT and other major providers offer you free weekend and evening calls, but if this is your dedicated business line you may not use it much at those times. There are plenty of special deals, such as 1899.com with which you put the digits (1899) in before the number when you dial. All national calls cost 3p to connect, but there is no cost for the rest of the call. International calls are also considerably cheaper.

Mobiles

Most people have one anyway, so when you start in business you might not need to do anything new. There can be a case for having a personal mobile and a work one so that you can draw the line between personal and work calls.

If you don't have a mobile or would like a separate one, you can choose between PAYG (pay as you go) which is still an excellent option for someone who doesn't use the phone all the time, or look for competitive contracts online. Having a contract means you get a good phone which is regularly upgraded, but even PAYG customers can get good deals on upgrading if they stay with the same provider.

Most phones enable you to have your emails directed to your phone and access to the Internet (provided there is Internet access). Some people think this is too intrusive, but others find it invaluable.

Mobile broadband

You can't always count on being in a wireless hotspot so you might want to buy a dongle to attach to your laptop to access the Internet. It's as small as a memory stick, but you have to sign a contract for your dongle, rather like a mobile phone.

The only thing to watch is that broadband connectivity is patchy and unreliable, even in big cities, so you have to think twice about the value of a dongle.

Again, you can get some good deals including pay as you go, so look at the mobile broadband section of price comparison sites.

Skype and other VOIP (voice operated Internet protocol)

Recent developments, such as Skype, are great for speaking to people abroad or in the UK, particularly if the calls are going to take a long time, as they are free of charge. Signing up for Skype is simple, free and can be done by going on to their website: www.skype.com.

Case study

'To be successfully self-employed you have to learn to pace yourself – time is money and you have to be highly efficient. If you are not careful you can find yourself working all hours and not being particularly productive.

'It's also important to be clued-up on computer software and technology. Because you have to do everything yourself you can save yourself a lot of time by knowing which programs can help you to run your business. Computers will not run your business, but they can be used as tools to reduce the amount of time spent on administration.

'I find that keeping an eye on the way others do business helps me to learn and try new things. Having an open mind is important too and I try to learn and develop new skills all the time so that my business moves forward.

'Business is like going to war – if you stand still you get shot. A moving target is always harder to hit, and there are competitors everywhere.'

Alan Parry, Roy Parry Associates Ltd, is a management consultant specialising in general business management, encompassing: marketing, sales, R&D, product development, manufacture, logistics and accounts.

'Computers will not run your business but they can be used as tools to reduce the amount of time spent on administration.'

Alan Parry, Roy Parry Associates Ltd.

Computers

It's personal choice as to whether or not you choose a laptop or a PC, or you might have both. Now that the computer is going to be for business use, its security needs to be even more important to you than when it was for home use. It is essential that it is protected from viruses and that you have the software that you need.

If you're buying a computer, don't go for the cheapest one you can find. You can get some great deals online or in-store with well-known names. If you are running a reasonable-sized business you will need a hard drive of at least 250 GB. You need not spend a fortune. Robustness and reliability are important, so look at well-known names like Dell, Sony, HP, Samsung or, if your industry requires it, you may need an Apple Mac.

What to look for:

- A hard drive of at least 250GB.
- A good-sized screen.
- A comfortable and well-made keyboard.
- Integral speakers.

When you become self-employed you lose the IT department of a large company. Now it is up to you to make decisions, and if you are not an IT expert you may need to find someone who is. If you have one in the family that is a great bonus, but if not you should ask other people in the area if they have any recommendations for local IT specialists, so that you know who to call if the computer crashes.

Backing up

There is also the thorny issue of back up. What happens if the computer hard disk crashes, there is a fire or your computer/laptop is stolen? You will lose all your documents and all your emails as well. Emails have become a complete filing cabinet of letters for most people in business. The chances are that many people do not have back up and would be completely lost if anything went wrong.

You could do one of the following:

- Copy everything regularly on to a disk or memory stick and keep it somewhere safe.
- Buy back up software.
- Try one of the online 'vaults' now available and free. You might first like to try your own provider or look at one of the main providers – BT, Yahoo, Google, Microsoft, which offer about 1GB (1,000MB) of storage.

Software recommendations

- **Microsoft Word** - a very advanced word processing and simple desktop-publishing package, essential for letter writing and general communication.

- **Open Office** - completely free, but check for compatibility with Microsoft if you need to send attachments to people, or transfer files onto another computer.

- **Microsoft Outlook Express** - an easy-to-use but very advanced way of managing incoming and outgoing emails, using a number of different email addresses for your business and personal requirements.

- **Microsoft Excel Spreadsheets** - can be used for simple accounts, costing sheets and databases.

- **Microsoft Office** - contains several MS packages, often including Word, Outlook Express and Excel.

- **Microsoft Access** - is a relational database within which you can write applications, building in a stock, inventory and valuation system or a customer database all linked together.

- **Adobe Acrobat Writer & Reader** - a very useful tool enabling you to develop copy and edit PDF files and send them as attachments to emails.

- **Adobe Photoshop** - this software opens and edits digital images in a very comprehensive way.

- **Sage Line 50** - can run your accounts and VAT (if you are registered), pay your suppliers and give you easily accessed management accounts to keep you in the black.

- **Ad Aware** - worthwhile to scan your computer for cookies that have been left when you visit websites, and it can block pop-ups.

- **AVG** - free well-respected antivirus and antispyware security software for Windows 7, Vista and Windows XP. www.avg.com

- **Skype** - free calls around the world, available free at www.skype.com

Broadband connection

Check out the broadband connectivity in your area before you set up office at home. Some more remote areas do not have good connections.

Don't go for the cheapest deals if you want fast and efficient broadband. For example, what you get for £5 is probably not suitable for a business. Check out what is included, because good prices often increase as you start selecting what you need. The best deals are for speeds of up to 8MB which is adequate for many home businesses, depending on your requirements. However, be sure to check exactly what you are getting, because up to 8MB could mean just 1 or 2MB, and it is preferable to have around 8.

If you don't already have broadband, again go for a recognised name and shop around for the best deal. Try one of the broadband price comparison sites:

* http://www.top10.com/broadband

* http://www.broadbandchoices.co.uk

To check speeds in your area put in your postcode and see what your neighbours are using, on this site http://www.broadbandspeedchecker.co.uk

There is also a company called Simplifydigital™ that do some of the work for you and give you the best deal for what you require. www.simplifydigital.co.uk Telephone (free): 0800 531 6350.

Shop around the well-known names such as: BT, Virgin Media, TalkTalk, Orange, AOL, O2, Tiscali, PlusNet, Sky and more. There are numerous good deals and you might find that you are being offered:

* Virus protection – this is essential to have, so if your broadband deal includes it, you are covered.

* Wireless router or hub – nearly all of them include this as part of the package.

* Phone package deals – free weekend/evening calls, etc.

* Television deals – available from BT, Virgin Media and Sky – broadband is tied in with pay-for TV. Check what you're actually getting – if you're a sports fan you may not get the right channels.

'Don't go for the cheapest deals if you want fast and efficient broadband. For example, what you get for £5 a month is probably not suitable for a business.'

- Free laptops and other goodies.

These deals may depend on where you live – for instance, Sky packages are not available everywhere

Wireless network

When you sign up for broadband you should receive a wireless hub as well to connect to your computer and enable laptops and other computers to run off the one broadband connection in the house (and it may even allow your neighbours to connect as well!).

Printers

Once again, choose well-known makes like Hewlett Packard (HP) or Epson. There are some cheap HP printers that combine photocopier, scanner and printer and can be very useful in a small office.

If you choose a very popular make of printer like Hewlett Packard you should be able to find cartridges in local stores when you suddenly run out and are in a panic!

Always check the cost of ink cartridges before you buy a low cost printer. If you print a lot you may find that you are spending a lot of money on cartridges. Check out cheap stationers such as Viking Direct online who make their own brands of cartridges or offer good prices on proprietary brands.

Case study

'I was in corporate life for over 30 years but after taking early retirement I set up on my own as a management consultant. One concern for me was that I had come from one of the biggest players in the broadcasting industry and wondered if I would be treated as seriously when I was no longer part of that brand. It was very liberating to find that I still had credibility in my own right.

'Having a high salary in a large corporate organisation means that you have to be prepared to work weekends and evenings and travel a lot, and there is a lot of pressure. Now that I am self-employed I enjoy having more control over my life and deciding when I work or which business trips I go on. I can decide to have time off during the day and work in the evening, and do not have to follow a 9 to 5 routine.

'For me the downside is that the administration is tedious – having to do tax returns, VAT returns, invoicing and keeping track of expenses wasn't all necessary when I was employed, as many things were just taken care of.

'In my industry I have to ensure that my knowledge is current and that I am up to date with new developments. I have to make sure I'm out networking because that's how I get most of my work. I can't get by on what I knew when I was employed so this has to be done in my own time, without the formal structure of a large organisation. It makes it interesting though and ensures that my work is not at all repetitive.'

John Ive, broadcast, video and IT consultant.

Summing Up

One of the most important aspects of many businesses today is the technology they use. Working remotely or on your own has become much easier with laptops, emails, Smart phones and the like. You need to purchase equipment and software that makes it easier for you to do your business, within the budget you can afford. Most businesses need broadband access, a telephone and a computer, but you should always shop around for the best deals that provide you with effective and reliable technology. Pay attention to the office furniture you use so that you are comfortable when you work and do not cause unnecessary strain to your neck, back and shoulders.

Chapter Six

Self-employed Status and Tax

The first thing to do when you start out is to register as self-employed with the tax office and get your unique tax reference number (UTR). It's important to decide on what your status will be in the eyes of the tax office.

For practical purposes being a sole trader is the easiest thing to do if you aren't sure what your earnings are going to be in the first few years. If you are undertaking a big project with a lot of risks involved, or can predict that your profits will take you into the higher rate tax bracket, you will be better protected if you form a limited company.

Banks are more likely to provide overdrafts or other funds if you have a limited company, and there can be tax advantages as well.

'Sole traders are more open to risks as there is no protection if you make a mistake and are personally liable to pay for it.'

A sole trader

The definition of a sole trader is:

- Someone who works alone without a partner.
- A business that is not limited.

If your profits are below the higher rate tax threshold it is more than likely that you will be a sole trader. Accountants usually advise people with higher profits to become a limited company to protect themselves.

Sole traders are more open to risks, as there is no protection if you make a mistake and are personally liable to pay for it. You are responsible for any debts that are accrued and your personal assets, which includes your house and other properties, can be seized to pay for them. This sounds rather severe but if you don't work in a particularly risky business, and many people don't, being a sole trader can be the best thing for you.

Advantages

- It is better for start-ups whose potential is not known.
- Offers more flexibility with scope to change later to a limited company.
- Less restrictions and regulations than for limited companies/partnerships.
- Less set-up costs incurred.
- The bookkeeping is less arduous, and less accountancy costs are incurred.

The lack of bureaucracy and formality suits lots of people well. If you are a freelance journalist, a beautician, a designer, a musician, a trainer, a complementary therapist, a yoga teacher or a window cleaner, it is more than likely suitable for you.

Employees

Employing people brings responsibilities too – such as setting up a PAYE scheme, paying National Insurance contributions and starting a pension scheme.

If you employ people who work full-time for you, you are obliged to set up a PAYE scheme and pay National Insurance contributions (NIC) for them.

If you employ five or more people through the PAYE scheme, you are obliged to set up a pension scheme for them.

A less expensive and easier solution is to employ people on a freelance basis, but you need to have evidence that they are self-employed so that you are not liable for their tax and NIC.

Insurance

All risks insurance/personal liability insurance might be necessary for people in business who run the risk of being sued if they make an error, but this doesn't apply to everyone. It is much more important if you are a lawyer or accountant or someone who works in people's houses, such as a joiner, electrician or plumber. If, however, you are a freelance journalist you are protected by the publications you write for who are responsible for content in their magazines, newspapers or websites.

Limited or not?

One of the most recent changes made by governments was the coalition's first budget in 2010 which made the corporation tax rate the same as that for individuals at 20%.

Your income can determine whether or not you are a sole trader or a limited company. The usual advice to anyone with profits over the higher tax rate threshold limit is to set up a limited company which protects you against debts and other liabilities.

Advantages

- A limited company is protected against debts and liabilities.

- You can pay yourself a combination of dividends from shares and PAYE, to avoid the higher rate tax threshold.

- It implies a certain status that could be important to clients/customers.

'The most common question that someone starting out in self-employment asks an accountant is "How I can pay the least tax?"'

Richard Kravetz, self-employed accountant and yoga teacher in north London.

Case study

'I have been self-employed for the majority of the last 20 years, initially after being made redundant, which made me feel that I'd like to have more control over my destiny. I like having greater autonomy too, so that within reason I can choose where I work and who I work for. If I'm not enjoying working with a client I can just grit my teeth and get through it because I know it will only be short term and I won't choose to work with them again.

'When I first started working on my own in a home office I found it particularly tough because I had come from a team environment. It was hard to motivate myself because I felt quite isolated, but over the years I have got used to it and actually enjoy my time in the office now. I also had to learn to become more self-sufficient. As I'd been in a senior role in my previous job, I wasn't used to sending faxes or even putting paper in the photocopier.

'It was particularly challenging having to find work and build up a client base. Opportunities turned up all the time and I used to put great trust in them, but only a small proportion of them came to fruition and people can mess you around. I had to learn to cope with rejection and as time has gone on I have become much more resilient.

'Overall, becoming self-employed was the right decision for me. However, it might not be right for everyone and it's important to go into it fully aware of all the challenges and potential pitfalls.'

Jane Lewis, trainer, coach and consultant in HR management and people development, director and joint owner of Recruit to Retain Ltd.

'When you are a limited company your salary has to be paid through the PAYE system as if you were an employee, although effectively you are employed by yourself.'

Paying tax

When you are a limited company your salary has to be paid through the PAYE system as if you were an employee, although effectively you are employed by yourself. There is an option to lower your tax bill by taking dividends instead of a salary, which enables you to save money on National Insurance contributions. Remuneration can consist of a combination of dividends and salary to minimise tax liability. Anyone expecting to have annual profits that are above the higher rate tax threshold should discuss options with a qualified accountant.

Directors

Often the owner is the only director and shareholder, but people may have their wives, husbands, partners, or other family members as directors or taking on the role of company secretary. The government is examining the role of spouses and other family members in limited companies, so it is increasingly important that they take an active role, and are not just there in name only.

Employees

Regular employees should be paid through PAYE, unless they are self-employed people who you contract from time to time, and who work for other companies as well.

The role of shareholders

The company is a separate entity from its owners, even if you are the sole shareholder, and in fact in a small company the shareholders and directors are often the same people. A company is owned by its shareholders, who may inject capital and purchase shares.

Administration

There is a lot more bureaucracy for a limited company than there is for a sole trader. A limited company is subject to company law, the Companies Act and accounts must be filed at Companies House.

In theory this means that full disclosure such as directors' remuneration, contracts received and other salaries should be included in the accounts, but most companies file abbreviated accounts which is acceptable and common practice. Less detail is required and the reason most companies prefer it is because the general public cannot have access to all your personal details.

Case study

ADPR Ltd was started by Alice Driscoll in the early 1990s. Now it has a team of 10 PR professionals working with regional, national and international clients. ADPR is now listed as a Top 5 south-west PR consultancy.

'For me, the change from self-employed to feeling 'employed' within my own company was a gradual process. At ADPR, we grew organically as the client base expanded, taking on more staff to handle the additional accounts we were winning. The hardest point was probably when there were only about three to four staff – at that stage you have to deal with all the legal aspects, tax, HR and personnel issues; and if you lose a member of the team it can feel devastating, and quite personal. I definitely still felt self-employed, but enjoyed having people around to share the load, enabling me to take a break occasionally and take on new challenges.

'Even though we were a limited company, the move to feeling "employed" came more as a mental change. It developed as we had the courage to take on higher paid and more influential staff, and set up a board of directors. This was as a result of using an external mentor in the form of a non-executive director, who has subsequently become my co-MD, and is active on the board. We've introduced an employee share ownership scheme, have regular management and board meetings, and now I really feel like I am employed by my own company. I'm not in the self-employed mindset anymore.

'As I have taken on more experienced and higher qualified staff, and got a board of directors alongside me, I feel I can free up my mind, worry less about the little things and move on to new challenges. That confidence comes with having people around you who are equally motivated to make the business a success and also who are better qualified than I am in key areas such as finance and HR.

'On the other hand, I worry about the welfare of the team, about the clients and the workload, about growth and potential threats. But I have had to learn to share and delegate, and overall it's definitely better for me now. Although I enjoyed being self-employed, I'm glad we've grown. I like change, and I like to feel I'm moving forward. To go back to being one key person with some support staff would definitely feel like a backward step.'

Alice Driscoll, ADPR Ltd.

Partnership

Lawyers and accountants have traditionally run partnerships which meant that if one partner defaulted and couldn't pay up, the liability passed on to one or all of the other partners. To avoid this, more and more law and accountancy practices have set up limited liability partnerships to protect themselves.

Partners

It can be helpful to have a partner with different skills, and this may be a brother or life partner. For instance, one brother may like taking wild risks and not be very good with money, but the other one is more cautious and takes control of the finances. This could save a business from failure.

Working with your life partner (husband, wife or partner) is very suitable in some ways because it's likely that you have already pooled your finances and feel that you can trust one another. The only problem with this is if you split up or divorce, it can threaten the business – although some couples are known to carry on in business even when they are no longer together in their private lives.

Basically, you need to be very sure of who you go into business with, and this probably has a lot to do with your own judgement and understanding of yourself. There are many friendships lost and family feuds due to being in business together, but there are also plenty of successes.

It is essential to draw up a well-worded agreement at the outset, preferably with a lawyer, which can lessen aggravation if you fall out. However, if disputes cannot be resolved the partnership eventually has to be dissolved, as opposed to a limited company which can carry on if one shareholder bows out.

Employing people

If you are employing people on a casual basis it is advisable to look for evidence that they are genuinely self-employed, otherwise you will be obliged to pay them through the PAYE scheme. In reality, a lot of people are in the 'black' economy, accepting payments without declaring them, so be sure that you are not implicated.

Case study

Sportsister was set up as a website about female sport in the UK. Unusually in this environment it started online and progressed to print as well, and now the magazine is distributed free through universities, schools, sports events, retailers and health clubs throughout the UK.

'I work in London but my partner on the magazine operates out of her office in Bath. One of the key things about working for ourselves is flexibility. Danielle can run her work around her children, on some days starting work after the school run, whereas I tend to work earlier in the day so that I can fit in the things I want to do in the evening.

'Of course, running a publication online and in print is stressful because I am responsible for the financial side, the content of both the website and the magazine, sales, managing staff, commissioning freelancers and IT. If I were a freelance journalist I wouldn't have all these responsibilities.

'The very nature of this title means that health, fitness and sport become integrated into my life. As far as possible we like to participate in the events we are writing about. For instance, I take part in swims and half marathons and have to train regularly, but this is the fun part of the job. Apart from editing the magazine I might be taking a box-load of magazines to distribution points, sorting out mail and emails, bookkeeping, or attending events. I get the opportunity to try out new fitness trends and recently had the experience of going in an altitude chamber at Bisham Abbey.

'It's hard to shut off from work at weekends or in the evening because ultimately it is down to Danielle and me, but I love the flexibility that working for ourselves brings us.'

Louise Hudson, editor and joint owner of Sportsister.

Self-assessment

A self-employed person needs to fill in a self-assessment tax return, as do some employees. As a self-employed person you pay your tax in arrears, and this also depends on when you started your business.

Self-assessment gives you flexibility to choose the end of your tax year – it could be the fiscal year end (April 5th) or at the time you started your business.

Tax returns

All self-employed people must fill in an annual tax return, including details of profit and loss, income from other means such as rental and pensions, dividends from shares, and building society and bank interest.

- If your year end finishes between January and April 5th you can include your accounts for that year in the tax return which covers the period from April to April the next year.

- If your year end finishes after April 5th you will be providing accounts for the previous year.

- If you have a profit of less than £15,000 you can fill in a short tax return, which is much easier to complete and does not necessitate using an accountant. The tax office will always help with any queries.

Dates for filing returns

- You can file your tax return on paper by 31st October each year and send it in the post to the tax office who will do the calculations for you.

- You can file your tax return online by 31st January.

There are financial penalties if you don't file your tax return by the final deadline (31st January).

'All self-employed people must fill in an annual tax return, including details of profit and loss, income from other means such as rental and pensions, dividends from shares, and building society and bank interest.'

Tax payment deadlines

- First payment due: 31st January, plus 50% on account for the following year.
- Second payment due: 31st July.

Payment on account

Earnings can go up and down and this can result in paying more tax some years and less the year afterwards. The tax you pay in January and July will also include a payment towards the following year – this is called 'payment on account'.

So if there is a profit of, say, £30,000 one year, the contribution towards the following year will be based on that figure. If you are having a worse year and your profit is likely to go down to, say, £19,000, you can appeal against the payment on account.

Always keep the tax office informed about what is going on – they are very helpful and if you are having a bad year, or even an exceptionally good year, it is worth asking them what you should do .

Managing tax payments

Paying tax in arrears may sound very appealing, but it requires a lot of discipline to keep the money to one side, particularly if your business is struggling. It is not uncommon for the self-employed to have spent all the money for tax by the time the bill arrives.

If you can do so, put a percentage of earnings in a special bank account and keep it there, so that you have the money by the time that the tax bill arrives.

VAT

Compulsory registration

The threshold at which it is compulsory to be registered for VAT is currently on a turnover of £73,000 – this is the total amount of money that comes in during one year.

Voluntary registration

You can voluntarily register if you earn less than the threshold, if you feel that it will be beneficial.

- If you buy a lot of equipment for your business it might be worthwhile.

- If use your car a lot for business you can claim some of the petrol VAT back.

- If your clients/customers are VAT registered, they recoup it. It will therefore make no difference to them if you charge VAT on your invoices.

On the other hand, if you provide a service to the general public you will have to include VAT in the price you offer, which could be a big disadvantage to you, as it could make your prices uncompetitive. Obviously if your turnover is above the threshold you have no choice in this.

VAT returns

There are various ways of submitting your VAT return. You will be sent a printed VAT return by HMRC according to which scheme you have signed up to, or you can file VAT online.

On the form you need to include:

- The VAT that you have charged to customers/clients.

- The same for EU business.

- The net amount charged.

- The VAT you are claiming back on purchases in the UK.

- The amount of VAT claimed back on EU purchases.

- The net amount on these purchases.

Flat rate scheme

Small traders with a low turnover, who are not obliged to register for VAT, may prefer to choose the flat rate scheme. This enables you to pay a standard amount at a lower rate than the current VAT rate, based on an assumption of how much VAT you are paying out each year.

Monthly VAT on account

You complete a VAT return every three months and you have one month to pay. If your VAT quarter ends on 31st March you must pay the VAT that you owe by 30th April.

Cash accounting

If you apply for the cash accounting scheme, VAT is only payable on amounts received, and does not include amounts that you have invoiced but not received.

Annual VAT returns

You can apply to only file one return a year, but you pay throughout the year on account – rather like a standing order for a gas bill which is adjusted once a year.

It is always worth talking to HMRC (see help list) because they are very helpful about VAT and other tax matters.

Needing an accountant

Because the short tax return is relatively easy and the tax office are particularly helpful if you have problems, you can get by without an accountant if you are in the standard tax rate band. Once you earn more than the higher rate tax threshold, it is preferable to have an accountant to do your annual accounts and tax return.

An accountant prepares your annual accounts, ensures that you are correctly claiming for everything you are entitled to, completes your tax return and advises you on VAT and filing returns.

Bookkeeping

Unless you have someone to do your bookkeeping for you, it is likely that you will have to do it yourself. Most people do this on spreadsheet software, but if you are not too keen on doing accounts on the computer you can use an accounts book, which is simple if your expenses are straightforward and you don't work for a lot of different customers/clients.

You could pay your accountancy practice to do your bookkeeping, but you might find it simpler to do them yourself because you have first-hand knowledge of your income and outgoings. Alternatively, your partner, spouse or other family member may do the books for you so that they are kept up to date.

It is essential to keep records up to date, or else it becomes a much bigger job preparing them retrospectively for your tax return.

This not only saves you money on your accountancy bill but it means that you are keeping a regular check on your outgoings and income, which is vital for running a viable business.

Keeping records

You, or someone appointed by you, needs to track monthly income and outgoings so that you can produce a profit and loss account for the tax office each year. There are various software programs that make this easier including: Microsoft Excel, QuickBooks Simple Start.

Records need to be kept for six years in case HMRC inspectors want to see them.

The main rules are:

▪ Keep all receipts for business, petrol, equipment, work contracted out, software packages, telephone calls, etc.

'You, or someone appointed by you, needs to track monthly income and outgoings so that you can produce a profit and loss account for the tax office each year.'

- Keep and file your receipts and bank statements by the month and year so that you can easily find them, and can present them to HMRC inspectors if required.
- Do monthly bookkeeping to keep on top of it, particularly if you have to calculate VAT for your VAT returns.
- Keep expenses separate from income.
- Take off VAT on invoices and expenses if you are VAT registered.
- The net expense is the figure required for your accounts.
- If you are not VAT registered use the gross figure in your accounts.

Typical income for one month when VAT registered

(VAT Rate 20%)

Date	Client	Gross	VAT	Net
9.4.11	Nutshell Co	£365.70	£60.95	£304.75
29.4.11	Bluewise	£705.00	£117.50	£587.50
30.4.11	T. H. James	£1,227.88	£204.65	£1023.23
	Total	£2,239.83	£373.30	£1866.53

VAT registered businesses

The net amount equals the expense when you are VAT registered. There are specific formulas for calculating VAT which can be obtained from HMRC or from an accountant. As VAT rates are subject to change the calculation is not included here.

Non-VAT registered businesses

If you are not registered you will not be claiming VAT back so the gross expense is the appropriate figure for your bookkeeping.

Being organised and having neatly kept records is beneficial for lots of reasons:

- If you have a visit from the taxman he will be satisfied that you are keeping a good record.

- If there are any queries about your income or outgoings you can easily check back.

- It makes it much quicker and easier to compile end of year accounts, even if you are just presenting figures to an accountant.

- It will save money on your accountancy bill.

Expenses

At the end of the tax year you will add up all the expenses and write them off against your income.

If you do not employ an accountant you should find out which expenses are chargeable and which are not. In general the following are chargeable:

Agents' fees and commissions

Motoring costs

The business use proportion of

- Road tax.

- Insurance.

- Petrol.

- Parking/congestion charges.

- Mileage allowance.

Telephone calls

- Landlines – either a proportion of the main phone, or the total costs for your business line.

- Mobiles – the proportion used on business.

- Broadband – can be totally charged as a business expense.

Office, shop or other work premises

- Rent of premises, office or serviced office.

- Mortgage interest on premises you are buying for your business, or a proportion of your mortgage at home if you are working at home. The proportion will be the room you use, and excludes all other rooms, so if your house has 10 rooms, it is only 1/10th.

- Electricity, gas, insurance, and other running costs as a proportion (say 10%, as above).

Equipment

Varies according to your occupation.

- You may need ladders if you are a window cleaner, cameras if you are a photographer, tape recorder for a journalist, etc.

- Computer hardware and software.

- Photocopier, fax, telephones.

- Office furniture – desk, chair, filing cabinet.

- Television costs – proportion of Sky or TV licence according to relevance to your occupation.

- Car – but note that the VAT paid on a car is not allowable as a VAT expense, unless you are (for example) a taxi driver or car hire company.

General office expenses

- Stationery, including cartridges for printers.
- Printing costs.
- Postage.
- Newspapers/magazines/books/CDs.
- Photocopying.
- Advertising costs.

Repairs/insurance

- Computer repairs or parts.
- Insurance for any expensive pieces of equipment.

Courses, conferences, associations

- Membership of associations, trade bodies, etc.
- Training courses.
- Workshops, seminars, conferences required for your ongoing professional development, or to do your job.

Travelling, accommodation, entertainment

- Provided you are away from home on business you can claim for subsistence (meals).
- Train fares, tube fares, taxis, when journeys are made for work purposes. Where possible keep receipts.
- You cannot claim for travel to and from work, but you can claim for travel to and from a client/customer's premises.

Outsourcing

■ Secretarial/clerical services.

■ Accountancy and bookkeeping.

■ Debt collecting or solicitor's fees.

■ Any other casual assistance.

These can be classed as business expenses rather than employee costs, provided they don't work exclusively for you and no one else, in which case they should be classed as employees and paid through the PAYE system.

Check the HMRC website (see help list) for expenses allowable for specific professions, such as clothing in some cases.

Note: if you charge expenses out to a client on their invoice, you cannot include them in your chargeable expenses. Also they are subject to VAT when you charge them out to your client, if you are VAT registered.

A typical entry in your records

(VAT Rate 20%)

Date	Payment	Supplier	No.	Cash	Bank	Gross	VAT	Net	Tel
3.4.11	Direct debit	BT	1		£45.60	£45.60	£7.60	£38.00	£38.00

Capital allowances

Your final accounts should include a figure for capital allowances which is calculated to reflect the writing down of equipment due to depreciation. You need to know when you bought the equipment and how much for, so keeping accurate records filed where you can find them is invaluable.

This applies to:

■ Cars.

- Computers.
- Office furniture.
- Office equipment.

Without any knowledge it can be difficult to work out your own capital allowance. You may need an accountant's advice, or you can contact the tax office (HMRC – see help list) who will help you.

National Insurance contributions (NIC)

You pay a lower rate of NIC when you are self-employed, and it is standard practice to pay this as a direct debit from your bank account.

Private pensions

The self-employed are not part of a company pension scheme, and even if they have paid into a private pension scheme, may find that the amounts payable are quite small. Private pensions got a bad name due to the fact that many don't seem to grow in size and lots of people who work for themselves haven't put much money into them.

This is purely personal choice – if, for instance, you buy a property as part of your business you may be securing a pension for the future.

However, if you are earning large sums it is possibly just as well to consider paying into a pension scheme, particularly as the state pension age is getting older and older. You will also receive tax relief on your private pension payments.

Note: If you employ more than five people you have to provide a pension scheme.

Summing Up

The first thing you must do when you set up as self-employed is to inform the tax office. You also need to decide what status you are going to be – are you going to be a sole trader, a partner or a limited company? It's important to do what is right for you and the industry you are in. You have to be responsible about bookkeeping, filing accounts to the tax office and paying taxes, including VAT. There is plenty to learn about doing your accounts yourself or you may wish to employ an accountant.

Chapter Seven

Coping With the Pitfalls

It is essential to be realistic. Can you do everything for yourself? Can you work alone? Are you motivated and disciplined enough? Be sure that you don't mind working alone, especially if you also live alone.

You must have an idea that is viable – if everyone you speak to believes you are doing the wrong thing, and you don't listen to them, you are taking a big risk. Conversely, some people can be negative about what you are doing if they are risk averse, so talk to business people and get some good feedback. And remember that many successful people were not taken seriously when they started out in business.

Use the services of local support groups such as Business Link (see help list), who will talk to you free of charge about your ideas. If they tell you it's unrealistic you may need to think again.

Above all you must be disciplined, able to take responsibility, know your own business very well and be prepared to work at odd hours. Working for yourself is supposed to give you a better lifestyle, so think about whether you will spend every hour of the weekend and evening working because you're such a perfectionist. Be aware if there could be peaks and troughs in your work when you can be bored, hard-up and stressed.

'Working for yourself is supposed to give you a better lifestyle, so think about whether you will spend every hour of the weekend and evening working because you're such a perfectionist.'

Most small businesses fail in their first year

This may not always be a disaster – it depends what constitutes failure. If someone decides to try being self-employed, doesn't earn much and goes back into employment it cannot be deemed as failure.

On the other hand, there are plenty of businesses who build up large debts and spend the rest of their lives paying them off. This is a situation to avoid at all costs.

Reasons for failure

- Cashflow is often responsible for putting people out of business – you have to pay suppliers, but your customers/clients haven't paid you, or you haven't invoiced them.
- Paying out too much when you buy an existing business or franchise.
- Crazy ideas – doing something that is not likely to work.
- Poor research into your market, your competitors and potential customers.
- Stock control – you have paid for stock but have not sold it, or you have insufficient stock and cannot fulfil orders.
- Customer service – poor relations with customers/clients, not listening to them, attending to their requirements, or responding to their requests.
- Skills – not having the right skills to do the job properly.
- Tax payments – spending all the money due to HMRC for tax or VAT.
- Moving with the times – staying stuck in the past, while competitors are moving on.
- Diversifying – not being creative and innovative if what you are doing isn't working.
- Marketing – waiting for customers and clients to come to you.
- Website – not having one when you need one.
- Non-payment – by clients/customers.

- Lack of focus – playing too much golf or nattering to your mates, and not focusing on the business.

- Bad debts – clients/customers going bust owing you lots of money.

- Insufficient funds – not enough money to keep going.

- Tough market conditions – which may well be beyond your control.

- Too much competition – from established players in your marketplace.

- Being lavish – buying smart cars, expensive computers, having lovely holidays and not concentrating on the bottom line of the business profits.

- Having your eggs in one basket – concentrating on one supplier leaves you vulnerable if they quit or go bust.

- Rising business costs – raw materials, outsourcing, often beyond your control.

- Changing markets – the Internet has revolutionised business which is detrimental for some.

- Borrowing too much and over-investment.

- Poor attitude to employees, sub-contractors, suppliers, customers and clients.

Online support

The European Commission Enterprise & Industry is aiming to support entrepreneurs in business with an online portal, entitled *A second chance in business*.

The web address is:

http://ec.europa.eu/enterprise/policies/sme/business-environment/failure-new-beginning/

Have you got what it takes?

☐ Do you know your market well?

- [ ] Have you done your research?
- [ ] Have you got the skills required to run your own business? Are you
- [ ] prepared to do everything?
- [ ] Are you comfortable with marketing and selling yourself or your company?
- [ ] Are you prepared to put in a lot of time and effort?
- [ ] Have you worked out the costs?
- [ ] Are you good with money?
- [ ] Have you carefully considered the location – is it appropriate for your business?
- [ ] Have you written a business plan?
- [ ] Have you got a marketing strategy and a website?

Over-expanding: employing people

'Often, a small business can be a victim of its own success – rapid expansion and taking on staff can lead to over-commitment.'

Something that happens to small businesses is that they grow fast and employ staff, and then when times get tough again they have to shed staff, costing them a lot in redundancy money. Often, a small business can be a victim of its own success – rapid expansion and taking on staff can lead to over-commitment.

Too much business

Alternatively, if you have more business than you can cope with you might not be providing a good service and your reputation could suffer. If your publicity has taken off so well that you are swamped with orders or requests for you to do work, you must attend to everyone who has contacted you.

If you have no resources to call on, explain that you cannot help them right now or that they may experience delay, but keep them informed. Perhaps this is the time to take on some casual labour to help you, or provide some short-term employment for family members – students are always keen to earn more money.

If your expansion shows signs of continuing then you have to evaluate what you can afford and either take on a member of staff or come to an arrangement with another self-employed person. Often others who are self-employed are only too pleased to do some work for their friends or colleagues to add to their own earnings.

Sometimes self-employed people do contra work with each other where they do work for each other, without any money changing hands.

It is at times like this that you may need to re-evaluate your systems, if you believe that a software program, for instance, would speed up work and help you to cope with the extra influx of business.

Finances

Your handling of finances must be really tight. Don't consider going out and leasing or taking out a loan on a car before you have even started. Be modest and carry on with the status quo. You need to know exactly what is coming in and what is going out.

It is not always your fault that finances go awry, because it can be due to bad payers. It's always helpful if you keep within your budget and don't take out huge loans to cover costs before you've earned any money. Alternatively, if you have funds to set up the business you won't need to borrow.

Inattention

You need to focus on your business to make it work – this doesn't mean to say that you can't have time off or work part-time. It is essential to do your research, know your market well and make big efforts to get business in. If you think of it as a hobby it will stay that way – this may suit you if you have a partner earning a lot or another income, but if you want to succeed you have to work for it.

Eggs in one basket

A large client/customer is brilliant for starting you off and ensuring that you have a regular income, but there is a tendency to concentrate on them and not try to get more business. Problems arise when they decide to take their business elsewhere or get into financial difficulties. If all your income dries up in one go, it may be impossible to continue.

In theory you should always be marketing and looking for new business, but this is easier said than done, especially when there is only one of you.

'It is not always your fault that finances go awry, because it can be due to bad payers. It's always helpful if you keep within your budget and don't take out huge loans to cover costs before you've earned any money.'

Cash flow

Since banks have been providing less funding and overdrafts, cash flow has become an even bigger problem for small businesses. There are various reasons why this happens.

- Invoicing – you must invoice on time and insist on being paid within your limits, which typically should be 30 days. Some industries expect to be paid up front, but in many service industries it is commonplace for clients to pay after 60 days or even more. This shouldn't be tolerated.

- Holding stock – if possible it is better to operate a 'Just in Time' practice, often used in manufacturing. This may not be practical but ordering stock when you have orders works very well financially. Holding stock can cause big problems because you may not sell it.

- Paying suppliers/staff – it is always the case that you have to pay your bills on time, particularly utility bills, tax bills; but no one pays your invoices promptly. Depending on the sums involved, this can cause serious concerns and cash flow problems and often puts people out of business.

The financial realities

The world could be your oyster and you may make more money than you could have dreamt of as an employee, but you may not. Self-employed people often have lower earnings than those who are employed, but they can have a better lifestyle.

You don't get holiday or sickness pay, and when you're out of work you may not earn anything. You are not entitled to government benefits, unless you completely give up and officially start looking for a job. You have to look after yourself in the bad times because you have opted out of the comfort zone of employment.

Case study

Adrian has spent most of his career employed, but has also had several spells of being self-employed. He recently set up Yellow Online Media, writing copy for newsletters and websites as well as being a journalist.

'I have had plenty of experience of being self-employed and am aware of both the pitfalls and the advantages. There is no doubt that one of the biggest plusses is complete freedom, but in this business you have to accept that it's either feast or famine.

'We all know people who just fall on their feet every time, but for the rest of us the breaks don't always come your way. You have to work hard, do a good job and be incredibly persistent. It's often about being in the right place at the right time, so if you don't get a job you have to realise that it doesn't mean that you aren't good enough, but that someone else was in that right place.

'I used to work for a large publishing company and was instrumental in bringing in big money, but when I am self-employed I am less comfortable with charging excessive fees, even though I know other people are doing so. When you work for yourself you have to be able to keep your finances in good order, knowing what is coming in and what is going out. You have to work hard at maintaining and creating contacts as no one else is going to do it for you.'

Adrian Bishop, journalist and web content writer of Yellow Online Media Ltd.

'Always make sure when you are asked to do a job, supply goods or work for someone that you have it in writing.'

Contracts and clients

In Britain, companies often do not pay on time. Work out how you will get customers and clients to pay immediately or quickly. The UK has no legislation about the length of time that invoices must be paid in and some clients take advantage of that, often waiting several months to pay their bills – it is often company policy.

Need2Know

Always make sure that when you are asked to do a job, supply goods or work for someone, that you have it in writing. This can simply be an email, but it still constitutes a contract, as does an invoice that has not been contested.

Better still, get a contract in which you can lay down your terms and conditions, such as payment times. Establish terms before you do work and do not rely on goodwill. It is better to ensure that your business has its own terms and that you want to be paid either at the beginning of any work you embark on, immediately, it is finished or within 30 days. Otherwise you will suffer with cash flow and your nerves can become frazzled.

After all, you have to pay the rent or mortgage and council tax on time or you get into trouble, but companies don't behave the same way. If you are in a business where you are paid up front, you should have much less of a cash flow problem.

You are entitled to add interest to bills when invoices aren't paid past, say, 30 days, but in reality it may be more difficult to get this money. The fact that you state this on invoices can encourage early payment.

Bad debts

Every now and then you won't get paid at all. The company you have provided goods or services to may go out of business. If it goes into liquidation the secured loans from banks and other similar outlets will receive their money before you do. The chances are you won't get paid. This is another good reason not to have all your eggs in one basket.

Before resorting to court action, keep on ringing and writing and consider getting a solicitor's letter sent – a Letter Before Action can sometimes do the trick and there is at least one company that charges only £2 (yes £2) for this plus VAT (see help list). You may find that a debt collection agency does the job for you, but weigh up all costs before incurring money.

Court action

If the amount is reasonably small you can go to the Small Claims Court without needing to pay a solicitor. You can make claims of up to £5,000 at Small Claims Court without incurring high costs, and without using the services of a solicitor. If you issue an invoice which hasn't been paid and no complaints have been brought against you at the time or later, it is more than likely that the courts will rule in your favour.

Many companies settle just before the court case because they do not want the bad reputation it could bring, particularly if the media get to hear about it.

Motivation

Not everyone who is self-employed is doing their profession of choice, but they are doing what they know they can do to earn a living. It can be very challenging to motivate yourself to do something that you don't really like doing. If you don't like your job you have a boss behind you making you get on with what you have to do, but who's going to tell you to get on when you are working for yourself? You need to be extremely motivated to keep going.

Case study

'Of course many people have dreams of things they'd like to do as a self-employed person, such as writing a book, or being a musician, or being an artist. While people do make a living out of these careers, the majority of us need to focus on work that will bring in money, while keeping our dreams on the back burner.

'I do try and practise what I preach, but I certainly know what the drawbacks are if I don't. I just feel down, depressed and stuck in a rut, whereas if I go for a walk, do some cooking, cleaning or gardening, it can sometimes balance me again, whereas staring at a computer when you're not in the mood can sometimes be a recipe for disaster.'

Linda Raymonde, events industry consultant.

When business isn't improving

When you've tried everything you can possibly try and you feel there's no more you can do, you may need to let it go. Sitting at a computer all day long waiting for emails and telephone calls can be debilitating and one of the downsides of working for yourself is that you could become quite depressed if you don't help yourself.

If you are confident that you have explored every avenue, made plenty of contacts and done all the groundwork and research you can do, there comes a point where you can't do any more.

Sometimes it is just a bad phase, but if it is getting you down, you could do some of the jobs that you have put off for ages – filing, sorting out your computer or your accounts, throwing out paperwork. Or even painting the house or office, going for a walk or playing sport.

All of this helps you to feel better and more focused, and while you're busy doing something else, the chances are that something will turn up

Most self-employed people who stay the course are very determined and accept the peaks and troughs. Some pick up other careers as well, diversify or try a new approach.

Alternative options

If things don't get any better you may need to consider your options.

- Look for a permanent full or part-time job.

- Look for contracts, temporary or freelance work to supplement your income.

- Add another career to the existing one – many people run two or three at the same time and can find that the one they set out to do is not the main one.

'Most self-employed people who stay the course are very determined and accept the peaks and troughs. Some pick up other careers as well, diversify or try a new approach.'

Handling stress

There are many things that you can do to help yourself if you are feeling stressed from underwork, overwork, or handling difficult people. When things go wrong you can feel trapped and completely overwhelmed.

- Regular exercise – it makes you feel good and helps you to focus. Whatever is your thing – running, yoga, tennis, football, tai chi, Pilates – it will make you feel better about yourself.

- Relax – whether it's meditation, reading a book, going for a walk in the countryside or lying down and closing your eyes, make sure you build it into your life.

- Talk – to a friend, your partner or even a professional if it is getting you down. Chances are that talking to someone will help, especially if you get to the core of how you are feeling.

- Read the Need2Know title *Stress – The Essential Guide*.

Case study

'I used to be employed as a pub manager but about 12 years ago I set up as a self-employed tennis coach which is much harder work, in that I have to put a lot more effort in. But if you put the effort in you get the rewards back, and being your own boss is a big bonus.

'There are downsides in that you don't get paid for holidays, so while you're away you're not earning, but you're spending money at the same time. Most of the time I work on outside courts, so the weather can obviously cause problems. When we had a lot of snow earlier this year I lost business for the next three months, because people normally sign up for a course in January, but they decided to wait until April. This is difficult for me as I still have children to feed and a mortgage to pay.

'I get a lot of business through word of mouth recommendations, but I still have to work hard to find and retain clients. When I'm extremely busy in the summer months from April to August, I employ other self-employed coaches and that works well.

'I have no regrets about being self-employed, particularly because I can choose to work when it suits me. I would never consider going back to working for other people.'

Cliff Porter, tennis coach, CP Tennis.

Summing Up

No one should be under the illusion that working for yourself is a bed of roses. It may offer you freedom, flexibility and control, but it can be enormously difficult. You have to make an income and in difficult economic times this may require nerves of steel and business acumen. Whatever your business is, you may go through lean times when you haven't got much business. It is important to be able to cope with this and think of other ideas and ways forward. There are several reasons why businesses fail and it is usually due to disorganisation, but there are plenty of things you can do to ensure that you make a living out of your chosen career and become successful.

Chapter Eight

Marketing Tools: PR (Public Relations)

PR is an inexpensive way of getting publicity for your business, if you do it yourself. If you are in a position to engage a professional firm or consultant for you, they will know how to approach the media and what will work best. You need to be sure, however, that you get value for money as some PR companies, particularly those in London, are very expensive and do not always put their most experienced staff in charge of your business.

There are plenty of freelance PRs who have extensive experience and cost a lot less, so it is worth advertising on relevant websites, or taking a look at directories to find someone, if this is the route you would like to go down.

If you do not have a budget for PR, it is something you can attempt yourself, but you need to take a professional approach. Bad PR can do more harm than good so take care to read up on it, talk to people, and consult Business Link, (see help list) or other organisations that can give you advice.

What is PR?

Public relations is about relating to your 'publics' – your target market, whether they are the general public, teenagers, car drivers, computer users, companies, or other self-employed people.

Good PR starts with how you answer the telephone, present yourself, and interact with people. What people first see will provide an image of your business – this might be your shop front or, nowadays, your website.

'Good PR starts with how you answer the telephone, present yourself, and interact with people. What people first see will provide an image of your business – this might be your shop front, or nowadays, your website.'

One of the most usual ways of obtaining good PR is to go through media that are appropriate to what you do.

How to approach the media

Step one: Media selection

One or all of the following could be relevant to your business:

- Local newspapers (weekly).
- Regional daily newspapers.
- National newspapers.
- Trade magazines.
- Consumer magazines (women's).
- Consumer magazines (specific hobbies or interests).
- Local radio/TV.
- National radio/TV.
- Websites.
- Social networking sites.

Step two: How to approach them

If you are dealing with local newspapers it is usually easy to get in touch with the relevant editor – the business editor, the travel editor, the fashion editor (whichever is appropriate). Before approaching the media be sure of what your 'story' is and why it will interest them.

Contacting national newspapers and consumer women's magazines is a good deal more difficult, as many editors no longer answer their phones. First of all establish who is the appropriate person for you to speak to, by asking the switchboard, or buying a copy of the paper where they may be listed.

Most national or regional daily newspapers and magazines operate all contact by email and prefer to have approaches made that way. This can be frustrating because you don't get an immediate answer or you may not get one at all, but it is frequently the way they like to do business.

Journalists are not gods, but on national newspapers and magazines they are literally bombarded with press information which they have to sort through. It goes without saying that they do not want to be hassled. Some will be polite about this, others will not and therefore it is better to be wholly professional about approaching them, even if it is not the way you like to do business. This is not advertising and it is up to the editors to choose whether or not to write about your business.

If you pester them they could decide to make a point of not using your material.

If they are interested, they will ask you to send a press release (see below).

Trade magazines, rather than consumer ones, which relate to your business, are much more approachable. They aren't so busy or so bombarded by callers, so it is often quite acceptable to call them.

Step three: Press releases

You must have something to send them when you speak to them. If they are interested they will suggest that you email a press release over.

A press release is written in a style that tells editors exactly what they need to know and allows them to contact you if they need more information.

Do not send (unless requested):

- Company or corporate brochures.
- Leaflets.
- Annual reports.
- Sales material.

'Journalists are not gods, but on national newspapers and magazines they are literally bombarded with press information which they have to sort through.'

If you do speak to the editor, the features editor, the news editor, a freelance journalist or writer, you have to have something ready to send them and this is a press release. Similarly if you are contacting a website or TV or radio station you need to send them a press release.

When you email them it is advisable to have a press release to send them in the first instance, to save them time contacting you and asking for one. It is often advisable to send it in the body of the email as attachments can be overlooked.

The purpose of a press release:

- To make your business recognised.
- To get the editor to want to publish what you have written.
- To interest the editor so that he/she wants to find out more.

Press release distribution

It is normal practice to send out press releases without ringing the editor in the first place. There may be 60 publications that you want to reach so you write a press release for them all.

Sometimes this is changed to suit the target. For instance, a national press release needs to be changed for your local paper so that it can be relevant – mentioning place names of Morgan Computers of Middletown, or even people, Bruce Jones from Middletown.

You may need different releases for trade and consumer publications – for instance, trade prices not retail ones, information about wholesalers as opposed to stockists and so on. Think about it carefully so that each type of media sector receives information tailored to it.

Post or email

Your choice really. Nowadays most releases go by email, but that means that news desks and editors receive volumes of them, and it's easy for yours to be overlooked. In theory, they will contact you if they are interested – in practice, they may never get to read it.

If you have a free sample to give away, send it by post with a press release – you just might be luckier sending it by post as it's less common.

Online press release distribution

There are now numerous sites through which you can put press releases out free. This means that your release can pop up all over the web and increases the chances of people reading it. See help list for details.

Social networking sites

Small businesses are using social networking sites more and more (see chapter 10, Digital Marketing).

Step four: How to write a press release

Information must be instantly accessible to give journalists the opportunity to accept or reject it in seconds.

First questions: How? Why? What? Where? When? Who? All these should be spelt out in the first paragraph:

- What is the subject?
- Who is the organisation or person/people?
- Where are they located?
- When is the event happening? (If relevant.)
- How is it of benefit and to whom?
- What date/time is the event? (If relevant.)

Other essentials:

- How much does it cost? What colour, size, availability? (If relevant.)
- Where to find out more – shop, website, elsewhere.
- *Always* include the date.
- Your contact details and the client's too – For further information please contact: Joe Brooks, 01779 840689, joebrooks@btinternet.com, www.powerpeople.co.uk

Heading

Tell the story in the first paragraph, keep it simple and don't try to write tabloid headlines. Make it to the point and interesting:

- Environmentally-friendly showroom to be opened by mayor.
- Innovative chair eases back pain.
- New software cuts bookkeeping time in half.
- £5 million contract awarded to . . .

'Tell the story in the first paragraph, keep it simple, and don't try to write tabloid headlines.'

Events

The most simple kind of press release announces an event:

'The Mayor of Tayville will be opening the new showroom at Bloggs & Co in Tottenfield on Wednesday, 14th March at 2pm The showroom has been designed to be environmentally-friendly and to show the company's extensive range of office furniture, which can prevent PC users from unnecessary strain, and backache . . . etc.'

Summing Up

PR is promoting your company to its 'publics' whoever they may be – the general public, dentists, IT specialists, bankers, car drivers, sports enthusiasts. One way of doing this is to get free publicity in the media, which is best done by a professional. Anyone running their own business needs to have an appreciation and awareness of PR and be aware of its basic principles. You need to identify the target media for your business and approach them accordingly. You need to have a genuine 'story' to tell the media, and present it in the accepted and professional manner without being pushy. They will make the choice as to whether or not they want to feature your business.

Need2Know

Chapter Nine

Marketing Tools: General

There are plenty of inexpensive marketing tools that you can use to get your business well known. By far, the best way of getting business is by word of mouth. People usually take more notice of a personal recommendation than anything else, so the more people who think that you are worth recommending, the better.

Although networking may sound like a buzzword, it is the most traditional way of doing business, that was in practice well before computers came to life. Networking doesn't mean pestering all your friends all the time, but appropriately maximising on opportunities to get you and/or your business known.

How to network

One of the best ways of networking is to have a wide circle of friends, associates and colleagues. In addition, you can join trade associations, networking groups, guilds, institutes and societies relevant to what you do.

Check out what there is in your area – for instance many counties or urban districts have their own regional organisations from development agencies to chambers of commerce, aimed at helping local businesses.

Find out what these organisations are through your regional Business Link website, who also put on their own events. Go to conferences and seminars, where the subject is appropriate to you – sometimes the event is of less importance than chatting to people who are attending it.

People do business with people, and it is by being known that you will get more business. The more people you know both socially and through business, the more likely you are to be recommended.

'People do business with people, and it is by being known that you will get more business. The more people you know both socially and through business, the more likely you are to be recommended.'

Always carry business cards with you and give them to everyone you meet at networking events, and everyone you do work for.

Some networking organisations take a very American approach which may not be for you. It's a bit like speed-dating where you dash around the room introducing yourself and exchanging business cards. It's rather impersonal and may not suit you, so find out before you go.

Alternatively, there are plenty of local networking organisations that can be found on the Internet or in local newspapers. You may find it more relevant to stick to your own industry for networking. Sometimes you meet competitors but you can also make useful contacts. See the help list for networking organisations.

Friends

It's great if you have a circle of friends who are also self-employed. You can support each other on an informal basis and you can talk through business issues together.

It's also a good idea with friends and acquaintances to do contra work – so that no money changes hands. For instance, you need some design work doing and the designer needs some help with their bookkeeping, or you get your hair cut for nothing if you write a leaflet for the hairdresser.

Essential but inexpensive PR tools

Some small businesses are very good at doing their own publicity. Others don't know where to start. There are many different ways that you can attract business and some of these can be done on a shoestring.

Leaflets

With computers it is easy to produce a well-presented leaflet which is aimed at getting people to contact you. There are numerous types of business which could benefit from producing leaflets, and they can be used instead of glossy brochures because they are much cheaper to produce.

'There are numerous types of businesses which could benefit from producing leaflets, and they can be used instead of glossy brochures because they are much cheaper to produce.'

Need2Know

Leaflets can promote:

- A new secretarial service for small businesses.
- A restaurant.
- A furniture shop.
- Accountancy or solicitors' practice.
- Estate agents.
- Freelance graphic designer.
- Computer repairs.

Leaflets need to be concise, to the point and they should convey exactly what you want to bring to the reader's attention. The English should be excellent and the presentation neat and eye-catching and they should make use of colour, bold type and capitals to make important points stand out. The example overleaf is similar to a leaflet being given out near a mainline station in London.

This leaflet was being handed out in the street to anyone who went past and as it is an extremely busy and buzzy area on a weekday, there were plenty of people there. The people handing out the leaflets spoke to everyone as they handed them out and pointed out exactly where the restaurant was.

- A simple, inexpensive way to publicise their restaurant with a well (yet cheaply) produced leaflet which is well written, and which makes the food sound enticing.
- It gives a feeling of freshness with delights made freshly for you and it makes your mouth water at the thought of Italian breads married up with the finest and freshest ingredients. Even the chips sound good as they are freshly made.
- Easy to read and enticing.
- People can't resist getting something for nothing.

The experience on the day must be good so that people want to come back, or it is a PR opportunity completely lost.

CAFFEITALIA

cordially invite

YOU

as their guest

to sample the many delights made 'freshly for you' on offer at the newly opened

CAFFEITALIA

the new concept counter service café serving 'baked on the premises' *Italian breads* married up with the finest and freshest ingredients and the best of *breakfasts*, freshly made *chips*, *cappuccinos*, *espressos* and *pastries*

at *115 Buckingham Palace Road, London SW1*

from

12 noon to 1 p.m.

Monday, 19th January

COMPLIMENTARY DRINK AND SAMPLE SELECTION available

Please bring this invitation with you!

Special offers

Not every leaflet has to incorporate a special offer, but if there is any way that you can do this it makes it more interesting.

■ Have your carpets cleaned before the end of January and take advantage of this 50% discount. (No one knows if they ever charge full price, but it has the effect of feeling that you're being offered a bargain.)

■ Sign up for 10 reflexology treatments and pay for nine! Again people feel like they're getting a good deal.

Prize draws

■ Bring this leaflet with you and you will be entered into a prize draw.

■ Bring this with you for a free glass of wine.

Make sure the special offer, opportunity to win a prize or whatever, is displayed prominently and use it as the headline:

■ Discount offer on pine furniture.

■ Free glass of wine at Bob's.

■ Win a bottle of champagne in the prize draw at Kandahar restaurant.

The following headline was on a leaflet distributed by a nutrition and skincare consultant who was keen to sell more products before Christmas.

Want to feel healthy, lose weight or just buy your Christmas presents?

The trick with the headline 'Want to feel healthy, lose weight or just buy your Christmas presents?' is that most people would answer 'Yes' to all of these. Most people want to feel healthy, and a lot of people feel that they need to lose weight particularly around Christmas, and virtually everyone needs to buy Christmas presents.

The leaflet was available at the salon, at an exhibition at which the consultant took a stand and they were delivered to houses within a mile radius of the salon. Although plenty went in the bin, this exercise cost the consultant very little. She designed them on her own PC, printed them and delivered them herself with some help from a friend.

Another way of making a leaflet look more attractive is to use coloured paper. It is easy to buy reams of coloured paper at one of the photocopying bureaux, or else order from a stationers. If you have the time and the expertise to make it look even better you can make a leaflet into a newsletter format so that it contains a variety of different items.

Quantifying results

It is one of the rules of marketing that you find out why someone came to you – always ask how they heard of you, so that you can track whether or not your publicity is working well.

Brochures

Lots of people believe that websites have taken the place of brochures, but is this true?

The answer is – it depends on your industry. The following are several reasons why you might need a glossy colour brochure.

- Look at what your competitors do – do they have glossy brochures?
- Is what you sell very visual? If yes, you may need a brochure so that people can see what they are going to get.
- If your customers/clients are just as likely to want to read a brochure as look on a website, you may need one.

Costs

There isn't a cheap way of doing a glossy colour brochure, so be sure you can afford it so that you can do it well. A poorly designed or written brochure will turn people away from you, not attract business.

It can cost thousands of pounds, so if you feel you need something, but cannot afford that, you may be able to have a cheaper produced leaflet. Be sure that this is appropriate for your industry though.

A brochure should:

- Be very visual with clear, well set-up photographs and images.
- Be professionally designed.
- Have plenty of white space so that it's not too cluttered.
- Have clear and eye-catching headings.
- Be professionally written with excellent English and *no* spelling mistakes.
- Be proofread by people who will spot mistakes.

Don't put anything in permanently which may change, such as the names and pictures of staff unless they are directors/owners. Loose pages in a pocket at the back could do this and allow for change.

The worst brochures include loads of information about staff and financial results which are not very interesting to consumers. It may be appropriate to include financial information if the company is in the finance industry, but otherwise it makes boring reading.

Mailshots and newsletters

A lot of businesses opt for email marketing as opposed to mailshots these days, but due to the volume of emails, including spam, that most people receive, this is not always the most effective way of marketing.

It may appear to be 'old hat' but sometimes a targeted letter still does the trick, and again this depends on your industry. People get less junk mail than they used to and because they are now more likely to be fed up with spam emails, they may be more receptive to approaches through the post.

If you would like to approach your local council, writing a letter may be very appropriate. If you are trying to approach companies in the Internet business, it is probably the wrong method.

You can send a leaflet, brochure or newsletter mailshot without an accompanying letter. The event management company newsletter overleaf was sent to PR companies to get more leads and increase business. They started

SNAPSHOTS

Volume 6 No. 3   Summer 1992
News from The Presentation Factor

300 Not Out!

1991 was a bad year for many companies, especially in marketing. How is it then, that The Presentation Factor has just completed its best ever year, a year which saw them organise their 300th event?

Production

Elaine Paige makes it a BIG Night

Petite Elaine Paige wasn't at all phased at starring on one of the biggest stage sets ever built at London's Grosvenor House Hotel for a private function. The occasion was Colonial Mutual's annual dinner for their top achievers. The complete event was designed and produced by The Presentation Factor.

Conferences

Hard work? Definitely. Dedication? Certainly. Ideas? Undoubtedly.

But what has really been the key to The Presentation Factor's success is service. "We were operating a 'service charter' long before it became popular with the transport and utility companies," says partner Elizabeth Cornelius. With five years' trading under their belt, The Presentation Factor has genuinely earned its reputation as a respected and reliable practitioner in the field of live events and presentations. "All our clients are equally important," continues Elizabeth, "so whether they are organising a small dinner for 25 VIPs or a major presentation to 1000 people, they can be sure of a first class job - whatever their budget!" Here's to the next five years!

Hale & Pace starring at a dinner dance organised and produced by The Presentation Factor for Grand Metropolitan

Christmas

We know it's only June but we are already planning a number of parties and gala dinner dances for clients' Christmas celebrations.

Call The Presentation Factor now to see how we can help with your plans for the festive season.

Roadshows

Dogs on Wheels

The requirement of animal charity, the National Canine Defence League, was for The Presentation Factor to design a fully mobile presentation that was eye catching and colourful, to promote the proper care of dogs to owners throughout Britain. The vehicle was to be used in shopping centres across the country.

News In Brief

Company Entertainment

Game, Set & Match to The Presentation Factor

Associated Leisure switched their allegiance this year from the Wimbledon Tennis Championships, where they habitually entertained some 40 clients, to The Presentation Factor. Could we devise a tailor-made event at which they might actually get to talk to their guests? Of course we could. The group got the VIP treatment, a specially chartered - and branded - plane whisked them to Reims to a sumptuous champagne tasting and gourmet meal in one of the region's leading champagne houses. "It was first class all the way," said one of the guests, bubbling with enthusiasm.

Dealers have a ball!

the trend of putting a little Post-It note on the mailshot with a handwritten note – These people look good – give them a ring! They got some significant business from this.

Courtesy of The Presentation Factor, www.presentationfactor.com

Delivering mailshots

If you know who you want to receive your leaflets, brochures or mailshots, you can deliver them or send them, but you may want to reach a wide audience of people you do not know.

If you have a specific market, such as PR companies or estate agents, you can probably find the information on the Internet, or in your local library, in the Yellow Pages in book form or on: www.yell.co.uk

Sending mailshots by post is inexpensive – if you send 100, you use 2nd class stamps and the cost is just above £30 plus the cost of the stationery which is minimal.

Magazine inserts

If you know your own marketplace – say, you want to reach all caravanners in the UK – you can pay a publication in this sector to insert your leaflets into their magazine. This can be quite costly but it ensures that every reader gets your handout.

If budgets are tight, you can spend much less. To get to every household or family in the area you can pop the leaflets through front doors which you can do yourself or pay someone in your family or some teenagers to do it. This way you can cover a lot of houses.

Other ways of distribution:

* Hand out in the street.
* Place on car windscreens (although this can irritate!).
* Pay the local newsagent to put them in with delivered papers.
* Put one up in the local newsagent shop or community noticeboard.
* Look for noticeboards at libraries, clubs, churches, village halls, colleges, and ask if you can leave one there.

Email marketing

Alternatively, you can send your leaflet by email, or one specially designed to fit in an email. There are many companies offering email marketing as part of a marketing strategy, but it is hard to say how many actually get read, if they don't go straight to the spam or junk filter.

Newsletters

Again, there are two types of newsletter – those in print and e-newsletters. You have to decide which is most effective for your business and which you can afford. Sending them by email is basically free apart from the time involved, but will they get read?

You can build up a database of customers, clients and/or interested parties, or subscribers on a website. It makes good sense to keep in touch with them regularly, to provide information, sell products, offer services, or just to keep the communication lines open.

If you already have a name with these people you stand more chance of having your newsletter read on email, particularly if they know when to expect it – e.g. on the 1st of each month.

Business cards

So simple but how often do people forget them or say they haven't got any? They are absolutely vital and these days they aren't that expensive. There are some companies who do business cards cheaply but put their name on the back, or you can go to local print/photocopy bureaux, which are not expensive.

Often it is worth having different cards for different purposes – they can be used as a publicity tool, not just with name and address details but perhaps just giving details of a website as below:

www.healthysoul.co.uk

Taking responsibility for your own wellbeing

Nutrition • Complementary Therapies
Women's, Men's & Children's Health
Infertility • Herbal Medicine
Environmental • Mind Body Spirit

feedback@healthysoul.co.uk

People should make good use of their business cards and routinely give several to people who are likely to refer them on. This applies to most businesses and it is essential to carry cards at all times to give out to people.

Price lists

Some businesses need a price list. If you run a beauty salon, people want to know what you can do and how much it costs.

To make the price list more interesting, each item can have a short description after it, such as:

- Aromatherapy – a relaxing massage lasting an hour and using a variety of essential oils to suit your own specific needs – £30.00.

- Computer Wizards – can service your PC or laptop, load new software, troubleshoot problems. Consultations start at £40 an hour.

Always put your phone number, email address and website on all communications.

Merchandise

Sweatshirts and T-shirts sporting company logos have become very popular in recent years and can be a good way of getting the message across. They are certainly good to be worn by you and your staff at special events, such as exhibitions, fêtes, or anywhere where people will notice you.

Alongside T-shirts and sweatshirts, you can have umbrellas, caps, pens, mugs, keyrings, bookmarks and any number of things with your company name printed on them.

It is an inexpensive publicity tool for a bookshop to give away free bookmarks with their name and address on them to customers. Sometimes the merchandise can be used in gimmicky competitions and given away as prizes.

'People should make good use of their business cards and routinely give several to people who are likely to refer them on.'

The message is to be sparing with giveaway merchandise and make sure it goes to the right people. It is sensible to let potential clients and visitors have company pens, particularly the inexpensive ones as the name continues to be publicised every time they use them.

It's not necessary to do all of these things, but to make a decision as to which is going to help you to gain customers and sales. Whenever you speak to anyone about your business on the phone or in person they are likely to say, 'Have you got something you can give me?' so a leaflet, a brochure, price list or business card is essential.

Summing Up

There is plenty you can do yourself to promote your business without spending a fortune. You are the most important asset you have, so move in the right circles, talk to people, do a good job, be recommended and join associations and attend appropriate events. You must have business cards, whatever you do, and you can produce leaflets and fliers on your own computer. Think of everything and you will find out what works for you. It may be appropriate to do a leaflet drop, or target people by email, send out a monthly newsletter, but make sure you do this regularly whether you are busy or not.

Chapter Ten

Digital Marketing: Websites, Blogging and Social Networking

Digital media now plays an important role in promoting businesses – i.e. the Internet, social networks such as Facebook and Twitter and blogging. Most people in business benefit from a website, but it isn't always essential.

What is a website for?

Many self-employed people operate websites as part of their core business. They may sell through them using e-commerce, or provide a service to the public or specific individuals, making money from affiliate marketing and advertising.

Many small businesses need to be seen to have a website which provides information about their services, as an online brochure. This might be a small – two to five page – website that can bring in business, so it is a marketing tool.

On the other hand, some people, such as hairdressers, plumbers, tutors or music teachers, may not need a website. They need local custom and often find that traditional methods of publicity work better – cards in shop windows, advertising in local newspapers and word of mouth.

What kind of website?

Decisions to make:

- Is it a 'brochure' website to sell your services and get people to know about you, but there is no direct selling?
- Is it a core business, from which you will be selling online or linking through to affiliates, from whom you receive commission on sales?
- Is it an information website, providing help and advice in a particular area of business/industry?
- Is it a magazine, the online equivalent to the print version?
- Is a website crucial to the success of your business?

Creating a website

'You should look at some websites that you like and formulate an idea in your mind as to how you want yours to look.'

Getting a name is very important – great if it relates to your business, or you may want to use your own name, or a cleverly worded name that drives traffic to your site.

Consider a name that includes the type of business – e.g. if you are working in travel it could be a name including these words – 'travel' or 'holidays' which is likely to get picked up by search engines when people are looking for holiday information.

You should look at some websites that you like and formulate an idea in your mind as to how you want yours to look. Look at those in a similar business to yours and think about what you can afford.

Then you need to decide who is going to design your website for you – you, a colleague or family member, or a web designer? Show them the websites you like the look of.

It's important to end up with a website you can update yourself, without ongoing costs each time.

Web designers

You definitely need to shop around for a designer, look at their previous work and speak to their customers. This will give you an insight into how they work, whether or not they are reliable and easy to work with.

Get quotes from at least three designers to compare with each other. There is a huge variation in charges, which should reflect the size and complexity of your site. The most basic website can cost as little as £100 from a small designer working alone, to large, complex sites that will cost thousands of pounds.

The advantage of employing a specialist company is that they can install all the extras you want, such as shopping carts, social networking links, advertisements and more.

If you are in a position to employ someone to host and look after your website they can do the work for you. You need to have some understanding of how websites work – for instance, you might be selling online, and you need to know about search engine optimisation using key words, and promotion online.

Read up about it and find out more through Business Link (see the help list) and other organisations.

DIY web design

Web design gets easier all the time, with simpler software packages available, so if you think that you could design your own website you could save yourself some money. You will need to allow time for the learning curve though. Nowadays you can do online courses or evening classes to learn how to create websites if you choose to design it yourself.

Google and other leading search engines take you through a step-by-step procedure to set up your own website for free. These are worth taking a look at if you only need a very small presence on the Internet, and there are other websites you can consult to find out how to do e-commerce. See the help list.

Essentials for a good website

- Clear, well written, concise and informative, with good spelling/grammar.
- Eye-catching and appealing layout and use of colour.
- Plenty of white space.
- Colour images.
- Not too busy.
- Consistent – with contents and other headings the same on each page.
- Easy navigation from one page to another, with lots of internal links, e.g. Read more about . . .

'There are hundreds of badly written websites with incorrect spelling and grammar, which creates a very bad impression.'

There is plenty to think about when setting up a website, particularly if you are including shopping and e-commerce. You will also have to consider where to put links, promotional messages and advertisements, and whether or not to get involved in affiliate marketing.

If relevant, you may need to consider the Equality Act October 2001, which relates to matters of religion, age, sexual orientation, disabilities and gender, when setting up your website.

Copywriting

The Internet has produced a lot of people who write, but they aren't necessarily good at it. There are hundreds of badly written websites with incorrect spelling and grammar, which creates a very bad impression.

Don't rely on spell checks because they don't pick up incorrect use of words – if you spell two as too, the spell check sees it as a correct word.

Ask someone you know who is good at English to proofread it for you.

Ask a journalist, copywriter or content writer to put the words together for you if you can afford it – web designers are not writers so don't rely on them, unless they have their own copywriter.

Look in the help list to find sites that give you access to writers.

In PR terms, your website is like your shop front and you will be judged on it. If it is messy, inaccurate, uninformative and difficult to navigate, it will turn away visitors and potential customers or clients.

Writing good content:

- Tell them what they want to know straightaway.

- Emphasise benefits to the reader, not features – what will they get from you, why do they want to employ you or buy from you?

- Keep it succinct, in short chunks.

- Make it easy to understand and clear.

- Use plenty of bullet points.

- Relate to them in a personal way, as people like to do business with people they feel familiar with.

- Don't include long documents or out of date data.

You need to think about who it is aimed at and if it appeals to them.

Only eight seconds

Don't write reams of information about yourself and why you are doing what you do. People get bored with personal histories and as the average amount of time taken to decide if they want to read more is around 8 seconds, you need to get the right message over immediately.

Services

If you are looking for clients/customers and you are offering a service, include a page of recommendations, quotes and/or testimonials from satisfied people. This often sells your service more than any other information.

Selling products

If you are selling products, you will need to consider how best to get people to the right page of the website to make a purchase. It should be as easy as possible, because they will quickly go elsewhere if it doesn't work.

You will need a shopping cart for them to purchase products, and this requires specific software which can be installed when your website is designed. If you start e-commerce at a later stage it can be incorporated then.

How will they pay for products?

- Through a payment processing company, such as Paypal.
- Through the shopping cart using specific software.
- With an Internet merchant account, which you need to set up through a bank.

Affiliate marketing

You can also sell services or products indirectly through other sites and receive commission. This is a much easier option than direct selling, because:

- You don't have to set up payment processes or shopping carts.
- You don't have to carry or pay for stock.
- You only receive a percentage of sales, typically from 5% to 25%.

How to set up affiliate marketing

- You can approach companies and see if you can deal directly with them. For example Amazon runs its own associate scheme so you communicate with them using your existing account details – email address and password.
- If companies belong to an affiliate marketing scheme, you can join free and choose which products/services you want to advertise on your site.
- You only receive set percentages of sales made through your website, but you don't have to pay anything.

- The banners (advertisements) can be copied from the affiliate marketing scheme website and installed on your site.

- When you sign up to an affiliate scheme you can select any number of affiliates according to what you do, and how many you want.

- The advantages of affiliate schemes are that you don't hold any stock or have to do deliveries. You just collect commission from orders via your site.

- It can take some work to promote these and you need to think of inventive ways of doing so. Some affiliate companies are very supportive and provide you with information, but some of them don't.

Search engine optimisation (SEO)

This is what everyone in the website industry talks about, so it's important for anyone operating a website to understand SEO, whether you are using the Internet to promote your small business or whether it is the very heart of your business.

Depending on the importance of your site to your business, you may employ a specialist company to market your website and work on getting it high up the search engines. The rules for SEO keep changing on the major search engines like Google, but specialists know what they are doing.

There are numerous companies specialising in SEO who you may like to use if you are in a good financial position. Be careful who you choose and go on recommendation, as there are many out there and some are better than others.

For many small businesses, paying for SEO may be an unlikely option in the early days, and you may well have to do it yourself. When creating the website you put in 'tags' or keywords which are most likely to get picked up by the search engines and bring people to your site.

Consider the following for SEO:

- The name of your website – will it reflect what you do and drive people to it?

- Make sure all writing is clear and correct.

- Use the company name within the text as often as is reasonable.

'It's important for anyone operating a website to understand SEO, whether you are using the Internet to promote your small business or whether it is the very heart of your business.'

- Place keywords or 'tags' throughout the copy. They should be specific – if you are in travel these are too general – 'red', 'fields', 'sea', but specific places like: Ios, Sorrento, or Niagara Falls, are likely to be more successful.

- Write copy focused on keywords.

- Link to other sites and vice versa.

Google and other leading search engines take you through a step-by-step procedure to set up your own website for free. These are worth taking a look at if you only need a very small presence on the Internet.

There is helpful information about SEO on the Business Link site. (See the help list.)

Promoting your website

You need to take an all-round approach to promoting your website, both online and offline. The first thing to identify is what the purpose of your site is:

- Is it a 'brochure' website promoting your services?

- Is it an e-commerce website selling products/services?

- Is it a magazine-style website, running advertisements and using affiliate sites to make profits?

Website for promoting services

Many people in business have to be seen to have a website. Therefore you should be putting your URL (web address) on all communications, including emails, letters, business cards, leaflets, brochures, etc.

This kind of website is not for entertainment value, but is aimed at potential clients looking for the services you offer. Therefore the kind of promotions that are appropriate to a more commercial site – such as competitions – are not likely to be relevant.

You want quality visitors who have a requirement for your service – you don't necessarily need thousands of them, but ones who are most likely to be interested in what you can do for them.

Commercial website

If you are using e-commerce and selling products (or services) your website should be focused on the core subject. Again, it is not an entertainment site, but one where people go to buy something (such as Amazon, for instance, where you go to buy books, DVDs and much more). Your aim is to drive people to your site and receive plenty of orders.

Entertainment/magazine-style website

You may be running a website where you are providing a lot of information – this could be a magazine-style website with articles, features and interesting news. You are most likely to be giving away information freely to whoever wants to read it, but there can be a money-making method – through affiliate marketing, or directly through advertisements on your site, or through membership to an organisation.

Your aim is to bring in a lot of visitors who will purchase through your affiliates or advertisers and accrue income for you.

Promotional ideas for websites

Many of these ideas are more appropriate for commercial websites.

Competitions

A regular competition can be successful at driving people to your site, but it will also attract people who are only interested in the prizes, and don't want to spend time browsing your site – there are many professional competition entrants!

This is particularly appropriate for magazine-style websites. It's relatively easy to get companies to give prizes away free, and you shouldn't need to pay for them. They may ask for the statistics of your site – how many people visit, and how many people you have as regular subscribers. The benefit to them is that they get free publicity for the duration of the competition, and if the prize is worth less than £100 many organisations are quite generous.

For instance, if you take the example of a travel website, you might find that you can get a spa day to offer your visitors when your website is relatively small. Don't expect to get a fabulous holiday in the Caribbean and flights until you can show thousands of daily visitors though.

Unless you clearly state it in a competition, you should not give people's names to third parties, as it contravenes data protection laws. If you claim in the competition that names/email addresses will be passed on to the company donating the prize, people can choose not to enter, or you could add an opt in/opt out button.

As competitions can attract the wrong sort of people, you might prefer to make it open only to those people who've signed up on your website.

Newsletters

Competitions give you the opportunity to capture some of your readers/visitors. You can make it a condition of the competition that they will go on your newsletter subscription list, but you must give them the option to unsubscribe as well.

Despite the people who are only interested in competitions, you will also have those who are genuinely interested in the subject of your website. It enables you to communicate with people who want to be kept informed and are regular users of the site.

The same principles apply to newsletters as websites:

- It should be well written with no spelling/grammar errors.
- Always better to employ a professional writer if you can afford it.
- Make sure it looks good, and is not too 'salesy'.
- Try not to include masses of links – I always delete those kind of e-newsletters.

A newsletter need not be expensive – if you do it yourself and send it by email there will be no costs. If you print it on your own computer/printer it will be a cost to you in cartridges. Obviously if you pay a writer to do the newsletter it could be more expensive – but charges vary so you may find someone who can do it for you cost-effectively.

Social networking

The rapid rise in popularity of Facebook and Twitter means that many commercial websites now link to social networking sites. You can put your business on Twitter and do regular Tweets that interact with your blogging. So, if you are in the travel business, you might send out Tweets about various destinations, or facts about holidaymakers, or statistics such as:

Did you know that France was the most popular destination for British holidaymakers? Find out why . . . or, Did you know that you can spend less than £300 and have a weekend in . . . ?

Social networking is not essential for sole traders whose core business is not on the Internet, although more and more business people use it as part of their marketing strategy.

Video marketing

To gain more publicity for your website and your business, you can make videos for YouTube. You can do this yourself and to find out how, create an account on YouTube, and you will find all that you need to know there. Alternatively, if you prefer to pay someone to do this for you, a web designer or digital marketing specialist could help you.

Videos can be incorporated into your website, blogs, Facebook and Twitter etc. (See the help list.)

Blogging

There are literally thousands of bloggers and some of them are writing for a very small audience, such as friends and family.

The purpose of a blog can be to bring traffic to your website, and can be linked to your social networking sites too. It's often great to have a voice in your industry, or to write about something unusual.

Clever blogging tells the reader something new and interesting, that they didn't know before, but entices them to know more, and to go to your website. It is effectively a sales tool when it is linked to a website that is a core business.

'The rapid rise in popularity of Facebook and Twitter means that many commercial websites now link to social networking sites.'

Digital marketing

The aim of all of these methods is to present yourself as the 'expert' in the field. You provide value because you are giving free information on your social networks and your website. If people trust the information and you, they are more likely to purchase services or products from you.

PR

The chapter on PR may apply to your website if it is a core business, although there are several things to consider. Other websites may agree to swap links with you, but they may not promote your website if it competes with theirs.

Approaching magazines or newspapers with press releases is certainly worth doing if your website is going to be of benefit to their readers. (See chapter 8, Marketing Tools: PR).

Summing Up

Most businesses have websites, but not everyone needs them. Decide what you need, how much you can spend on it and whether it is core to your business or just a way of promoting your services. A website needs to look professional with good design and sales messages. It should be well written as well as appealing to the eye, and if it's very important to your business you will need professional help, unless you are an IT expert or are planning to learn web design. It may be important to blog regularly and be registered on social networking sites to add further promotional opportunities.

Help List

Business advice

The British Chambers of Commerce

65 Petty France, London SW1H 9EU
http://www.britishchambers.org.uk (www.chamberonline.co.uk)
Chambers of Commerce in each city or county provide business support,
courses and training and opportunities for networking if you become a
member. Find your local Chamber of Commerce from the above website.

The British Chambers of Commerce advice on business start-up

http://www.thebusiness-startup.co.uk/

Business Gateway

www.bgateway.com
0845 609 6611
Advice and support for new businesses in Scotland only.

Business Link

01845 600 9006
www.businesslink.gov.uk
Plenty of help and detail on their website with factsheets available on all
aspects of setting up a small business, from finance to tax, and websites to
office space.
Contact your local Business Link for help, details of seminars and to make an
appointment to discuss your business.

Business Wales

www.business.wales.gov.uk
Free advice for businesses set up in Wales.

Citizens Advice Bureau

http://www.adviceguide.org.uk/index/life/employment/self-employment_checklist.htm
Direct link to CAB's advice page on self-employment. The Citizens Advice Bureau can provide legal advice and information about regulations for free.

The Department for Innovation and Skills (BIS)

www.bis.gov.uk

The Federation of Small Businesses

The National Federation of Self-Employed and Small Businesses Ltd (FSB)
Sir Frank Whittle Way, Blackpool Business Park, Blackpool FY4 2FE
Tel: 01253 336000
www.fsb.org.uk
Campaigning pressure group that lobbies parliament on behalf of the self-employed. Membership available.

Highlands and Islands Enterprise

www.hie.co.uk
Business and community support specific to the Highlands and islands of Scotland.

Northern Ireland Business

Tel: 03000 603000
www.nibusinessinfo.co.uk
Support for new businesses, existing businesses and those that wish to relocate to NI.

Prince's Scottish Youth Business Trust (Scotland)

15 Exchange Place, Glasgow G1 3AN
Tel: 0141 248 4999
www.psybt.org.uk

The Prince's Trust

18 Park Square East, London NW1 4LH

Tel: 0800 842842
www.princes-trust.org.uk

Shell LiveWire

Tel: 0191 423 6229
www.shell-livewire.com
Worldwide organisation for young entrepreneurs aged 16-30.

Smallbusiness.co.uk

Tel: 0207 250 7010
www.smallbusiness.co.uk
Advice on how to set up and run a small business, with help on technology, banking, tax, where to work and much more, plus a Q&A page.

Small Firms Enterprise Development Initiative

SFEDI, Business Incubation Centre, Durham Way South, Aycliffe Business Park, County Durham DL5 6XP
Tel: 0845 467 3218
SFEDI is the government recognised UK Standards Setting Body for Business Support and Business Enterprise. Run by entrepreneurs for entrepreneurs, SFEDI researches leading practice, sets standards, principles and guidelines.

Financial & tax advice

HMRC (Her Majesty's Revenue & Customs)

http://www.hmrc.gov.uk/selfemployed/
0845 915 4515
Advice on how to register as self-employed, what forms to fill in, what to do tax-wise, and much more. The website is a mine of information for the self-employed. Telephone lines are open: 8.00am to 8.00pm, Monday to Friday, 8.00am to 4.00pm, Saturday and Sunday, closed bank holidays.

Money Saving Expert

www.moneysavingexpert.co.uk
Run by Martin Lewis, who has made a thriving business out of giving advice
online on how to save money, get bargains, and live within your means. Advice
on redundancy and ideas on how to find work and boost your income.
Also advice on what to expect from your state pension and projected payments:
http://www.moneysavingexpert.com/reclaim/state-pension

Funding

Angel News

www.angelnews.co.uk
Website that puts investors and entrepreneurs in touch with each other.

British Business Angels Association

The New City Court, 20 St Thomas Street, London SE1 9RS
Tel: 0207 089 2305
www.bbaa.org.uk

Debt collecting

Small Claims Court

www.hmcourts-service.gov.uk
Small claims courts and advice. Business Link also provides advice.

Thomas Higgins Solicitors

Debtor Direct Fax Line 0151 514 2108
Debtor Direct Phone Line 0151 514 2109
www.thomashiggins.com
Thomas Higgins Solicitors charge just £2.00 + VAT for a Letter Before Action,
which can often do the trick.

Business and freelance work opportunities

The British Franchise Association

http://www.thebfa.org/

Self-regulating body for franchising, with members who are franchising companies. Plenty of advice on franchising.

Freelancers in the UK

www.freelancersintheuk.co.uk

Freelance projects for accountants, bookkeepers, illustrators, copywriters, event managers, researchers, hairdressers, photographers, etc.

Freelancers Network

www.freelancers.net

Freelance positions for graphic designers, programmers, copywriters, proofreaders, sales and marketing professionals.

Gorkana

www.gorkana.co.uk

Jobs and freelance projects advertised for PR professionals and journalists.

Gumtree

www.gumtree.com

A variety of jobs in a wide range of categories, both permanent and freelance.

Netmums

www.netmums.co.uk

Parenting website with excellent advice on working for yourself, franchises and direct selling job opportunities.

Network Freelance

www.networkfreelance.co.uk

Freelance jobs for PR, marketing, SEO and copywriting positions where employers are put in touch with freelancers.

People per Hour

www.peopleperhour.com
A bidding site where freelancers put in a bid for specific jobs and the client chooses who to employ. Covers projects in media, design, event management, finance, research, administration, IT, etc.

Source that Job

www.sourcethatjob.com
Freelance projects and job adverts for PR professionals and journalists.

Women Like Us

http://www.womenlikeus.org.uk
Mostly part-time jobs, but some contract employment too. A helpful website with information for women looking for work.

Networking

The British Chambers of Commerce

www.thebusinessnetworkonline.com
Networking through Chambers of Commerce.

Business4Breakfast

www.bforb.com
Business networking around the country and events, plus franchise opportunities for the organisation.

Business Networking International plc

BNI House, Church Street, Rickmansworth WD3 1BS
Telephone: 01923 891999
Fax: 01923 891998
www.bni-europe.com/uk/index.php
Business networking events for members. Dynamic style.

Ecademy

www.ecademy.com
Business networking online and in person with regular events.

Everywoman

www.everywoman.co.uk
Free membership, plenty of resources for women, annual conference, and details of numerous local networking groups for women. Publish own books.

Simply Networking

www.networking4business.com
Local events and networking.

Online social networking

LinkedIn

www.linkedin.com

Business social networking

Facebook

www.facebook.com
You can add a business facility to your Facebook account.

Twitter

www.twitter.com
You can do regular tweets and run business news through Twitter, when you've signed up.

Office furniture

Argos

www.argos.co.uk
Reasonably priced office furniture.

Ebay

www.ebay.co.uk
Where you can bid for office furniture/equipment, or Buy It Now at set prices.

IKEA

www.ikea.com
Stylish but cheap office furniture.

Viking Direct

www.viking-direct.co.uk
Office furniture, stationery and equipment at reasonable prices.

Telephone calls

1899

www.1899.com
Cheap calls if you put the 1899 code in before you dial. National calls cost 3p
to connect and free per minute.

Skype

www.skype.com
Free calls worldwide to people who have signed up to Skype. Facility to pay for
calls to mobiles and landlines.

Mobile broadband

Broadband Genie

http://www.broadbandgenie.co.uk/mobilebroadband/

Top10.com

http://top10.com/broadband/mobile_broadband/

Online back up storage

Google

https://docs.google.com

Business cards

Vistaprint

www.vistaprint.co.uk
Business cards in a variety of designs. You only pay for postage, but Vistaprint's name is on the back. Facility to pay more for different designs.

Website Design

Google

www.google.co.uk

The UK Web Design Association, UKWDA

www.ukwda.org

E-commerce

International Advertising Bureau

http://www.iabuk.net
For information on how to get started with e-commerce.

Online payment processing

Paypal

www.paypal.co.uk
The most used payment processing service, which is secure for both supplier and buyer.

Press release distribution

A selection of online press release distribution sites – all free.

www.clickpress.com
www.enewswire.co.uk
www.freepressreleases.co.uk
www.free-press-release.com
www.newsmakers.co.uk
www.pr.com
www.pressbox.co.uk
www.prfire.co.uk
www.prlog.org

Book List

Balance Your Life and Work
Everywoman Books, £6.99, www.everywoman.com

Daily Mail Tax Guide, Jane Vass
Tax Handbook (2010/2011), Which? Essential Guides

Employer Further Guide to PAYE and NICs
Available from HMRC in a variety of formats and is a very comprehensive guide.
http://www.hmrc.gov.uk/guidance/cwg2.pdf

Work Well from Home
Everywoman Books, £6.99, www.everywoman.com

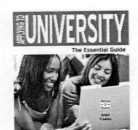

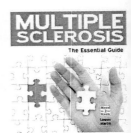